# Twenty Life Lessons

# Twenty Life Lessons

A MEMOIR

———

*Lawrence Abrams*

No Harm Press
New York, NY

ISBN: 0692766340
ISBN-13: 9780692766347

Library of Congress Control Number: 2016913210
No Harm Press, New York, NY

# Author's Note

———

MY STUDENTS AND COLLEAGUES KNOW me as someone who cared passionately about my craft when I was a principal and teacher. Now, as I turn 70, it is time for me to use my words to reveal lessons from my life. This book is dedicated to my loving daughter Meredith who through the years has given me everything I could have wanted without my ever having to ask.

As a grandparent, I feel the pressure of time to compile a written legacy designed to encourage both continuity and change within those who read its pages. It is my wish that my daughter will share this memoir with my grandchildren, Charlie and Dexter, when they are old enough to understand how to live a good life.

# Reader's Orientation

———

TWENTY LIFE LESSONS IS ABRAMS'S blueprint on how to lead a good life. Each chapter is designed for readers to judge the beliefs and values expressed. This introspection is especially important considering the vast social and political divide currently plaguing our country. People on both sides of the schism are dissatisfied and need to look inward before they can effectively communicate with each other.

This memoir has two voices. The first is a child who discovers the government suspects his loving parents of being communists. The second is a grandfather, trying to explain to his grandchild how to achieve the safety of a good life. Abrams weaves the effects the government's institutional persecution of his parents and the subsequent choices he made to protect himself and those who he loves. The insights are "lessons" in human dignity.

Using his grandparents' FBI files, Abrams reinvigorates our current debate over national security and civil liberties. His skills as an educator and story-teller empower the reader to assert a common humanity which is in sharp contrast to the bullies and demagogues who wish to amass power, instill fear and stymie change.

# Acknowledgments

———

*TWENTY LIFE LESSONS: A MEMOIR* is edited by Miriam R. Haier with photo editing and the back cover photo by Carolyn Ciarelli.

# Contents

# Larry Abrams's Family Tree

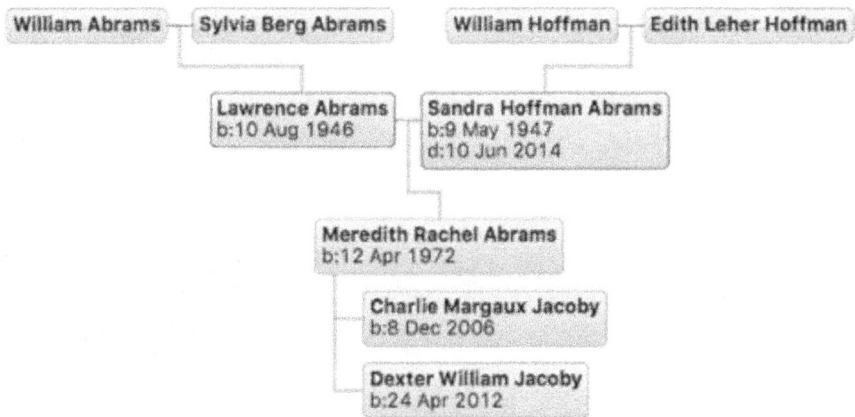

William Abrams — Sylvia Berg Abrams    William Hoffman — Edith Leher Hoffman

Lawrence Abrams
b:10 Aug 1946

Sandra Hoffman Abrams
b:9 May 1947
d:10 Jun 2014

Meredith Rachel Abrams
b:12 Apr 1972

Charlie Margaux Jacoby
b:8 Dec 2006

Dexter William Jacoby
b:24 Apr 2012

As you view the following photographs of four generations, think of the picture of Charlie and Dexter as an oil painting. A pentimento is a trace of earlier painting that is visible through newer layers of paint on a canvas. If the life lessons in this book are understood, they will seep through and provide this painting with a rich, unexpected texture. The resulting image will be that of a good life.

Charlie & Dexter

Larry, Mer & Charlie

Sandy & Meredith

Grandmas & Children

Larry & Sandy

William & Edith Hoffman

William & Sylvia Abrams

Sylvia Abrams

William Abrams

# On Television

"HEY, LARRY, CAN YOU HEAR me," my mother would yell. I couldn't, because it was Tuesday night between 8 and 9 P.M. and I was glued to the television set in our neighbor's apartment. Mrs. Schurin was kind enough to invite us to watch television in her 80 Winthrop Street apartment on the fifth floor. Television was new and we didn't have one yet. Every Tuesday night for *The Texaco Star Theatre* featuring Mr. Television himself, Milton Berle, I would sit mesmerized, cross-legged, and two feet in front of the flashing black-and-white images appearing on the cathode ray tube screen.

The show would start with male gas station attendants singing the Texaco jingle.

> Oh, we're the men of Texaco
> We work from Maine to Mexico
> There's nothing like this Texaco of ours!

> Our show is very powerful
> We'll wow you with an hour full
> Of howls from a shower full of stars.

We're the merry Texaco men
Tonight we may be showmen
Tomorrow we'll be servicing your cars!

Then Uncle Miltie would come out and do his Catskill shtick. I was so far in a zone it didn't matter what he did. I found it funny. It is like young kids today when given a smartphone: They instinctively know how to caress the keyboard with their thumbs and download all sorts of stuff which will hypnotize them for hours. Technology changes, but people's infatuation with media does not. To think, all the time I wasted in high school learning keyboarding so I could type with all ten fingers.

A few years later, my mom and dad bought our own television set. At this time we lived in a one-bedroom apartment. The Zenith Console television with its rabbit ears antennae opened up my world. I was no longer in Flatbush Avenue, Brooklyn, but in a whole new dimension. Howdy Doody, Mister Bluster, Buffalo Bob Smith, and Princess Summerfall Winterspring were my new friends. I longed to be in their audience, dubbed "The Peanut Gallery," and see Clarabell spritz some unsuspecting guest with his seltzer bottle.

Since I was allergic to dogs, I could now share in *The Adventures of Rin Tin Tin* and bellow the command, "C'mon Rinty," whenever I was in a tight situation. I became a Video Ranger on *Captain Video* and even wore a decoder ring so I could decipher the secret message at the end of the program. I was not a great fan of *The Mickey Mouse Club*, though when Annette Funicello appeared in her Mouseketeer costume, it did hold my interest. For cowboys I watched *Roy Rogers*, the singing cowboy, and later wondered whatever possessed him to have a taxidermist stuff his horse Trigger. Would his wife Dale Evans's horse, Buttermilk, be subject to the same fate? I could watch George Reeves play the mild-mannered *Daily Planet* reporter Clark Kent, whose alter ego, Superman, was faster than a speeding bullet and stronger than a locomotive when fighting for truth, justice, and the American way. The *Winky Dink and You* show had nothing to do with truth or justice, but you could put a plastic film up on your TV screen and use a marker to trace shapes from the cues on the television set. What could be better than that? Perhaps, Miss Molly on *Romper Room* or *Kukla, Fran and Ollie*, when Fran Allison had her gentle, understanding conversations with the hand puppet Oliver J. Dragon.

With all these childhood media fantasies, there were two instances when the images on the picture tube crossed into real life. First was when the service station attendants on *Texaco Star Theatre* had young boys sing the theme song. Fifteen years later, I worked with one of those singing boys, named Larry Strickler, who at that time was a new social studies teacher like me at Sheepshead Bay High School. Larry liked teaching and parlayed his musical talents into a second job becoming the social director at The Brickman's Resort in the Catskill Mountains. I spent many a summer visiting my wife Sandy's parents in a bungalow colony in Wurtsboro, and visiting Larry and his wife Shelley at The Brickman's Resort. Larry still remembers the jingle and his moments of fame when his voice, in chorus, entered into all of America's living rooms.

The second instance was a bit more ominous. One day there were three harsh knocks on our apartment door that broke my concentration from watching one of my favorite TV programs, *I Led Three Lives*. My mother answered it and I went back into my viewing cocoon, not paying much attention to the two men who were speaking with muffled voices to my mother and father.

*I Led Three Lives* was like a cowboys-and-Indians show, where the good guys triumphed over the bad guys by the end of each half-hour. The lead character, Herbert Philbrick, was the good guy: an FBI agent who put himself at risk by going undercover. Much like Superman's alias Clark Kent, Philbrick fought for truth, justice, and the American way. He did this by subverting intricate, evil communist plots to take over America. He was a husband and advertising executive in life one, a member of the Communist Party in life two, and an FBI counter-spy in life three. He did his job in such a way that the evil communists never suspected he was a double agent.

The TV series, starring Richard Carlson, was loosely based on Philbrick's book of the same title. In the book he joined the Massachusetts Youth Council, which advocated peace. Later the group was a front for the United States Communist Party. In an obituary in *The New York Times*, Philbrick is quoted as warning America about the dangers of the Soviet Union and communism during The Cold War in the late 1940s and 1950s. He said, "The free world is shrinking and the communist-controlled world is growing. It's the old salami tactic, one slice at a time." (I should mention that Philbrick was from Boston, because if he were from

Brooklyn, a "salami tactic" would have quite a different connotation, especially if it were an old salami.)

A power vacuum existed after Europe was devastated by World War II. The two superpowers vying for world power were the United States and the Soviet Union. Many Americans don't remember that Russia was our ally in World War II, and it wasn't until after the war that mistrust vested itself in the American spirit. Then the Soviet Union was "God-less," and Americans feared that the Red enemy would destroy our Christian civilization with atheism. Senators like Joe McCarthy were using communism to scare Americans into believing that witch hunts were necessary to root out the communist devils in our free society. McCarthyism became defined as "the practice of making unfair allegations or using unfair investigative techniques, especially in order to restrict dissent or political criticism." People who were the targets of investigations were blacklisted and could not get jobs. Thousands of Americans were brought before committees that tested their loyalty by asking them to incriminate others to save themselves.

It was a time of conformity; those whose thoughts deviated from the norm were shunned. Few people spoke up for their fellow Americans' civil liberties, fearing the Senator's power. It was a time when many in the free press remained silent. Before McCarthy's downfall, J. Edgar Hoover, the Director of the Federal Bureau of Investigation, realized he could amass great power by making the public aware of the communist threat and then having the FBI effectively combat alleged communists to prevent them from infiltrating strategic industries, smuggling drugs, stealing secret weapons, and, worst of all, corrupting America's youth.

Director Hoover was keenly aware of public relations and chose to review the scripts of the TV show *I Led Three Lives* to ensure the image of the FBI was properly crafted. For example, in *The Fiancée*, Philbrick checks out a pretty brunette taking the same communist indoctrination course he is. Her fiancé happens to be a scientist working on a top-secret project, and the FBI is convinced that the sweet brunette is stealing classified information and passing it to a contact in the class.

In other episodes Philbrick's palpable risk of exposure as an FBI agent is ever-present as he sneaks into secret communist cell meetings, exposes plans to convert vacuum cleaners into bombs, and foils assassination attempts. What a terrific show. The bad guys always got what was coming to them and I, as an American, was safe from those evil communists who wanted to take away my freedom. God bless the FBI, J.Edgar Hoover, and super-agent Herbert Philbrick.

Then again, there was that knock on the door that my mother answered. I found out later that it was two FBI agents who came to bring my father in for questioning because he was suspected of being a communist. My mother told me to go on with my daily life and not tell anyone. As I looked around our empty apartment, what other choice did I have? My father was gone, and all I could see was my mother's distressed face. The TV screen was immersed in black-and-white static that echoed my pulsating anxiety.

# On Experts

———

YOU ARE MY GRANDCHILD, AND it has come time for me to sit you down and tell you what I know. Together we will look at the choices you might have and see how to make them into a good life.

However, we have a problem. I am old and you are young, and if I were to tell you everything I know, your head would surely explode. It would probably only be the top part of your brain, above your eyebrows, so you would see it splatter all over the kitchen table.

Then we would think, "What a mess we've created!" and go to the paper-towel-holder under the cabinet to clean up your brain splatter before anyone could see it. With love, I would carefully pick up the pieces, strain them, disinfect them, pat them dry, and begin the jigsaw puzzle of putting your head back together again in the best order possible.

Even before you could look at me with your adoring, innocent eyes that sparkle with joy, I would wave my hand and say, "There is no need to thank me. This rearranging of splattered brains before anyone notices is simply what grandfathers do."

Truth be told, even with all my degrees, there are many people who know more than I do. These people are called "experts" because they know a great deal about specific areas. I have heard that many experts become full of themselves because they know what should be done and what direction to take. If they lived on a grid, they could with great confidence say, "When I come to a corner, the best thing to do is turn right." They could follow the plan until they ended up walking around the block again and again.

Though these experts develop great knowledge of everything within the square block, some never dare to turn left. Left is different. Left is unknown. Left is something to be feared. If you turn left, others may not accept it. Some experts have nervous breakdowns if they make the wrong turn. It leads to a path out of their comfort zones. It leads to a place where they are no longer experts and have to accept the fact that they are just as lost as everyone else. They no longer have their status to comfort them.

The one thing I know is that I am not an expert. There are already too many self-proclaimed gurus in this world, making a good living advising people what to do and how to live. You see them all the time, promoting themselves as the solution.

I prefer to know as little as possible. This way when I come to a corner, I can be curious about which path to take. Curiosity is what makes life worthwhile. I see that trait when I look into your eyes.

Don't be scared when you choose which way to go. Constantly have adventures that take you to the places you want to be. In the following lessons, I will be your Sherpa, helping with the baggage on "the road less travelled." I wish that forever and always I could walk that road with you, to guide and protect you. Sadly, I cannot.

# On Lefties

APPROXIMATELY 50 YEARS AFTER THOSE strange men came to speak to my parents, I mustered the courage to obtain my father's file from the Federal Bureau of Investigation using the Freedom of Information Act. My mother and father trained me not to speak about anything political that might land me in trouble, and as a good son, I complied. After my father died I had a need to find out more about him—which is not an uncommon feeling for people who have lost a parent—and my sisters and brothers had different memories of what had happened and why. They knew that many Jewish intellectuals like my father were attracted to the left as a result of the wealth inequalities ever-present after the Great Depression. On December 8, 1941, the FBI recommended that my father be placed in "Group A." That group is for "individuals believed to be the most dangerous and who in all probability should be interned in the event of war."

I was born in 1946 and ever since then my father had been the most gentle and loving with me. One time my Uncle Sam took me to Ebbets Field to see my Dodgers play. It turned cold and nasty. At the end of the game, thousands of people came steaming out of the stadium. There was my dad waiting for me with a warm sweater. How could he be anything but a loving father? Yet Herbert Philbrick had a life no one knew about. Was it possible that my father had a secret life too, perhaps as a spy for the Communist Party—someone Herbert Philbrick might have foiled? What would the FBI's 373-page dossier reveal?

According to the dossier, Simon Weber, who worked for *The Jewish Daily Forward*, first told an FBI agent that my father was a danger to American security. *The Freiheit*, where my father worked, had more leftist views than its rival paper *The Forward*. Weber claimed that William Abrams was not my father's real name, but he did not know the real one. Weber asserted that my father "also travelled to Russia. He is simply a writer for the paper. He was at one time the City Editor and also held other positions in the paper, but no longer holds any of them. He probably is illegally in the United States. He usually lives in furnished rooms. At one time his was on East 18th Street, somewhere between Second and Third Avenues. It is understood he is paying alimony to about three wives." It was this interview that started the ball rolling for the FBI to arrest my father.

William David Abrams was my father's true name. He was also known as Wolf Abram, which is a derivation of William Abrams. At *The Freiheit*, he used the pen names Slim Willie, Welwel Abrams, David Marba, David Mayerson, and William Mayerson. It seems that *The Freiheit* wanted to impress its readership that it had large staff, so one reporter had numerous incarnations. My father did travel to Russia—not for any clandestine meetings, but rather on assignment from his newspaper. He was also searching for his brother and remnants of his family. His brother was a Communist Party official who was sent to Siberia.

My father entered the country legally on the S.S. Maine in Baltimore, Maryland, under the name Wolf Abram on December 7, 1912. He re-entered legally on May 26, 1930 on the U.S.S. Ballin. On September 25, 1943, he filed his Petition of Naturalization #497295, but his petition was denied.

He was married to his first wife, Rose Weiner, with whom he had two children—Carl (b. January 22, 1919) and Nina (b. May 18, 1921)—and granted a divorce from Rose on October 16, 1944 to marry my mother, Sylvia Berg. In the interim he spent nine years in a common law marriage with Leah Gessler, resulting in the birth of my half-brother Robert in April of 1934.

Carl, Bob & Larry

My mother always told me with a smile that she insisted she would have a ring on her finger before she had me. The fact that he was paying alimony of $25 a week (when he could afford it) would have been considered a good thing in some circles. I remember many celebrations with my half-brothers and half-sister and their families. Though we were not "Ozzie and Harriet"—the archetypical American nuclear family of the time—we had our moments.

Extended Abrams Clan

The FBI noted that on May 5, 1916, my father was charged with grand larceny for stealing a wagon-roll of clothes valued at $100; however, he was released within a day when the real culprit was found. The charges were dismissed on May 10th by the grand jury. His other legal infraction was that in 1940 he smoked a cigarette on a subway, for which he paid a fine. Neither incident seemed to threaten national security.

My father did admit to the FBI that he had been a member of the Communist Party from 1919 to 1922 and when he joined *The*

*Freiheit* in 1924 to 1943. (Apparently the FBI suspected the head of *The Freiheit* was a representative to the Jewish Bureau of the Communist Party.) Over time my father found the communists too dogmatic and he wanted a Zionist State, which was opposed by American communists. In fact, the party indicated he was *persona non grata* because of his long-term and outspoken views on the future of the Jewish people. He became disillusioned and severed his ties.

To my knowledge, which includes all of the information in his FBI dossier, never did my father advocate the violent overthrow of the United States government. On May 14,1945, and then again November 1947, the New York Office of the FBI recommended that there was no reason to maintain my father on the Security Index, which listed people who may be a threat to America in times of war and should be interned. J. Edgar Hoover himself responded from Washington, D.C.: There was to be no rest for anyone with leftist leanings. Even though the FBI could not make a criminal case, they continued to investigate.

During these times, there was little difference between "prosecute" and "persecute." If there were no criminal charges to be filed, perhaps my father's immigration status could be used to get him to talk—hence the knock on the door, rudely interrupting my viewing of *I Led Three Lives* and leaving my mother devastated but too protective to show it to me.

The FBI would move my father to an immigration detention center and threaten him with deportation unless he named names. The authorities made it clear that in order to regain his freedom and return to his wife and child, my father would only have to cooperate in this way. The FBI had worked in concert with Immigration, conspiring not to process my father's naturalization papers, and now his state of limbo would serve as a fulcrum to trap others in guilt by association.

# On Sunlight

———

HAVE YOU EVER LOOKED AT the sun? What color is the light? Is it the bright yellow you see in a child's picture, or is it transparent, with no color at all? Does it make what it shines on more beautiful or less?

Imagine for a moment that you are a prisoner in a dark cave with no light at all. You are there bumping into other prisoners and grunting without even saying, "Excuse me, I am sorry I bumped into you." (People at this level should have a name. Let's called them "stoopid" with two "o"s.)

People in this cave eventually discover fire, but then all they can see is their shadows on the cold, murky walls. Sounds of prisoners moving echo in the cave's crevices and make it seem that the sounds are coming from the shadows on the walls. In reality they are coming from the prisoners, but no one is bright enough to figure that out. (People at this level should also have a name. Let's call them "stupid" but with a "u" instead of two "o"s.)

Let us say you are one of the prisoners in the cave who dares to be different. You look at the fire directly. At first, it hurts your eyes, but as they adjust you start to see things more clearly than before.

Other people who are too afraid to look at the fire don't see things the way you do. They grunt, "Look away from the fire if you know what is good for you."

You do not. Finally, you see a small path leading out of the cave that the others cannot see. You climb slowly and carefully so as not to stumble and fall. As you come to the cave's opening, you see your first sunlight. A part of you wants to return to the safety of the cave and its fire, but you do not. You choose to go on. You choose to see things as they really are.

The sunshine enlightens everything around you, and its warmth enlightens you too. You discover a simple truth: sunlight = knowledge.

If ever you decided to return to the darkness of the cave, your eyes would no longer be able to adjust to the darkness. Other prisoners in the cave would think you'd gone blind in trying to escape their world. "Look what happens when people don't follow the rules," they would chant. "We need to kill anyone who does not believe in darkness. Look what happens to your vision if you leave the safety of our cave. You go blind and stupid." You would hear these people and they would frighten you.

Now you need to ask yourself a most important question. Would you try to escape again? Would you seek truth and knowledge in your life no matter what the cost?

These are not my questions but are those of a man named Socrates, who was a Greek philosopher who lived from 470 to 399 B.C.E.

His student Plato (429 to 348 B.C.E.) probed these concepts in "The Allegory of the Cave." I have adapted them so you can think what form you might like your life to take. If there are indeed ideal forms of knowledge, truth, goodness, and beauty in the world, then how will you recognize them? How will you lead the good life?

LESSON 5

# On Integrity

———

WRITTEN ON THE GREEK TEMPLE of Delphi around 1400 B.C.E. are the words, "Know Thyself." Later Shakespeare wrote, "To Thine own self be true." If you think about it, these are the same thing. Your wisdom is what gives you substance. Should you compromise yourself to gain your freedom?

I continued to read the FBI dossier fearing that my father, like so many others who were subject to the fear tactics of McCarthyism, was going to name names to save himself. My brother assured me he wouldn't have because he had integrity. But how did my brother know? He wasn't there, and now I was the only one in possession of the historical record. And even if my father had named names, could I blame him, given the circumstances?

It was on May 23, 1949—four years after the knock on the door— that a memo was sent to the New York office of the FBI to cancel "the Security Index card" of William Abrams. However, the FBI was authorized to interview—or in this case, re-interview—the subject. The interview, it said, should be conducted by "two experienced agents well versed in Communist matters." The agents interviewed my father and recommended that the Immigration and Naturalization Service be informed of the results of this interview. "In view of the uncooperative attitude of Abrams and the unproductive nature of the interview, it is felt that no further contact should be made with him. It is also suggested that the Immigration and Naturalization Service be informed of this interview and of Abrams's attitude." The translation is: He told us nothing of value, and we have no criminal case, so perhaps Immigration can find something to disrupt his life and deport him.

However, even though my father did not cooperate, the FBI believed in the motto, "If at first you don't succeed, try, try again." The FBI suspected that my father was the espionage agent known only as "Ben." An agent showed a picture of my father to a self-confessed former communist and espionage Agent who clearly stated my father was not Ben. The only similarity between Ben and my father was that both were described as having thick lips; otherwise, no resemblance. Confidential informants at the Chicago FBI office were solicited to make a connection, but there was "no identifiable, disloyal information" as of July 25, 1952. The Philadelphia office and Los Angeles FBI offices were contacted but yielded the same results as Chicago.

The memorandum of June 13, 1953 shows that Ben may have known Bessie and Joseph Katz, the owners of the alligator articles company Tempus Imports, where my father was briefly employed. Joseph loaned my father $1,000 to start a leather goods company called the Meyriv Trading Company. Joseph Katz was Menke Katz's brother. Menke was a well-known Yiddish poet and best friend to my father. There, the trail ran cold. There was no connection between Ben and my father. Because this lead didn't pan out for the FBI, the government's espionage case was impossible to make, and they knew it. Instead, the government decided to arrest my father as an "undesirable alien" on October 17, 1951. After a hearing, he was recommended for deportation.

My mother, Sylvia Berg Abrams, decided that enough was enough. She borrowed money from her brother Sam to hire a lawyer named Mordecai Merker to represent my father in defense of the "undesirable alien" deportation proceedings. In the appeal Merker argued that my father was not a communist within the declared meaning stated in the McCarran Act, and that the Immigration and Naturalization's testimony of William Abrams taken on December 6, 1948 was not properly transcribed and that my father had signed it without reading it. The FBI files indicated that the copies of the testimony taken December 6th were destroyed.

There was another confidential informant known as T8 who said he had known my father since 1933 when he was a Communist Party member and employed by The *Morning Freiheit* and attended Communist Party and social functions with him. In 1945, T8 was informed that Abrams was on friendly terms with the employees of *The Morning Freiheit* who were communists but was thrown out of the Communist Party and was now operating a costume jewelry business. T8 was told not to have anything further to do with William Abrams. T8 described my father as an "intelligent individual but was very lazy and would not apply himself unless he was interested and felt work was benefitting his talents. His disposition was that few people could get along with him." The translation is: He was kicked out of the Communist Party for not listening or parroting the party line.

This informant also added, "Abrams had the ability to get along with women and always had three or four 'on a string.'" I was hopeful that this ability to get along with women would be passed on to future male generations. As for the "three or four women" statement, informant T8 probably got that right. My father was a handsome man, and my brother Bob and sister Nina would tell me that women were always attracted to him. I remember he once told me with a slight smile, "Son, a woman is like a bus. If you miss one, another one will come along in five minutes." Today this advice sounds sexist or egotistical. When he said it, it wasn't; it was just how he found things.

It should be mentioned that my father had long-term relationships with three women: Rose, Leah, and of course my mother, Sylvia. When Leah died, my father and mother became my brother Bob's legal guardian. In May 1952, Bob came from Los Angeles to live with us in our one-bedroom apartment, 4E at 80 Winthrop Street. These actions seem counter to the government's version of my father as a "deadbeat dad" with a loose lifestyle.

Prior to the Immigration and Naturalization hearings, the FBI agents were very thorough in their investigation. They monitored our phone calls, checked our mail, and used whatever information they found to investigate anyone and everyone my parents had contacted. Banks were also monitored. They investigated people from whom my mother or father borrowed money.

Uncle Sam Berg

In their investigations, the government discovered that my Aunt Pauline Attkiss had once joined the Communist Party in 1945 under the name "Pauline Atkins." My Aunt Pauline gave her sister Sylvia $1,000 so my father could make bail. She did not have a political bone in her body. However, rather than seeing the loan as one sister helping another, the FBI interpreted this act of generosity as an international Jewish conspiracy. My mother's brother Sam also gave her $4,000 for my father's bond, and he was thoroughly investigated, too. My Uncle Sam swaggered into his interview saying, "I want you to know I am not a communist!" He owned his own pharmacy in Merrick and was a big fan of capitalism, but he was also a fan of his sister who was in need. Even the superintendent of 80 Winthrop Street was interviewed. Mr. Albert Dacres said, "The Abramses are quiet tenants." In this surveillance approach, the message was clear as could be: This family is under investigation, so beware if you don't want to be investigated too.

My father found it very difficult to secure employment because of the FBI's whispering campaign. I remember a series of leather watchbands, and later nickel gumball machines that my father owned to try and support us. At one time it was hairbrushes. My mother would stroke the brush through her hair and say, "This brush is really expensive," to which my father would groan disapprovingly. For a short time my father worked for The United Jewish Appeal earning $40 a week as a fundraiser. Most of the time, he could no longer find work and spent his time trying to translate his Yiddish novel, *I Sew and Sew*, into English. Our apartment 4E rented for $53 a month. My mother worked as the manager of the Sheepshead-Nostrand Public Housing Projects in Brooklyn which housed approximately 1,800 families. She earned $6,170 per year. Luckily, she was a civil service employee, which helped somewhat insulate her from the FBI's pressure.

I benefitted from the efforts of the FBI in a strange way. My father had always been working as his other children were growing up. While I was growing up, he couldn't find work, so he was totally in my life. He was a good father and a gentleman, curiously loved by all of his children from his previous marriages. Because I was there with him, I became his favorite. He would take me to

Prospect Park or the zoo and would talk to me about what he read in *The New York Times* each day. He bought me six-ounce bottles of Coca-Cola from the cooler in the local candy store and could finish a bottle in one gulp. He loved taking me rowing on the lake in Prospect Park, and I can still hear the squeak of the oars in my memory. I can still see and smell the bottles of Canadian Club—the popular rye whiskey at the time—that my father and his friends would drink when they came to the house celebrate their lives. There was a joy in the air and a feeling that life was worth living, counter-pointed by my father's quiet idleness from not being able to find employment.

Here is the bottom line: My father admitted to having been a member of the Communist Party but stated that he broke with them when they violently advocated the overthrow of the United States government. He was a member of MIR, a Jewish writer's organization, and the International Worker's Organization (I.W.O.), which provided insurance for members of The Newspaper Guild. Every two months or so he spoke for the I.W.O. regarding literary matters. The House Un-American Activities Committee saw the labor movement around New York City as being hijacked by Jewish intellectuals. Anyone who wanted to make the workers organize for better rights might be considered a communist.

My father was proud of his firstborn son Carl, who joined there United States Air Corps and completed 50 missions in World War II. He wrote an article of praise entitled, "My Son, The Bombarder." Later the FBI decided to investigate Carl for his theater interests at Camp Unity, another link in the international communist conspiracy. Eventually Carl was blacklisted as a radio writer and as a result made a career for himself as an advertising executive at McCann Erickson.

My father did know communists at *The Freiheit* and in the labor movement. He chose not to name them, in stark contrast to the choice the employee of *The Forward* made to name him. In the end, the FBI found him uncooperative, which I consider a good thing. He spoke of his own activities honestly but could not recall specific facts when they wanted him to "report" on others—much to the annoyance of FBI investigators. He paid a heavy price in terms of his own arrest and unemployment, but in the end he held his head high.

In reading his dossier, I was very proud of how he reacted in times of personal stress. He possessed the simple gift of integrity. He knew himself.

# On God

—

ONE MORNING, BEFORE SUNRISE, YOU awaken in a state between dreams and consciousness and hear a voice call to you. You can't tell if it is a male voice or female voice, but it will sound like an important voice all the same. It will call to you by name.

At first you are too afraid to answer, but after a deep inward breath, you say, "Who are you?"

The voice replies, "I am God."

"Okay," you say, "But why are you here?"

God replies, "I am here to see if you will recognize me and let me in."

Frozen, you reflect for a minute upon the request. Should you let Him or Her in?

Many people have, and in so doing have found comfort in their lives. They pray, confess their sins and try to live a good life by following religious teachings. They build a spirituality in a belief larger than themselves and share with a community who also believes in that spirituality. They believe God has created the universe by some intelligent design.

Others believe that God did not create man but that man created God as a way to explain things he does not know how to explain. People fear death and they wish to go on and on and on in a place they can be happy. A belief in God assuages their fears and gives people hope they will live on. If they live well and follow the rules of the religion, they are rewarded; if not, they are not.

You think quietly to yourself, "Do I want to be one of these people? I want to be good, so which religion should I choose? Mommy is Jewish, Daddy is Catholic—should I pick one of these? Or should I do something completely different and become a Buddhist or Muslim or Protestant or Hindu? There is so much from which to pick. What shall I do?"

"I am waiting," God says, "and I can wait forever; however, you need to choose what will make you the best person you can be."

As philosopher Friedrich Nietzsche put it: "Is man merely a mistake of God? Or God merely a mistake of man?"

By now you are completely awake and not sure what to do next. Like smart grandchildren, you go to your grandfather, whom you call Poppy. You relate your experience and ask, "Poppy, what should I do?"

Poppy looks at you straight in the eyes, knowing you have asked him one of life's most important questions. "I can't tell you that," he says. "I can only tell you how I answered this question."

Your great-grandparents on my side were Jewish but did not believe in God. They believed it was important to be Jewish and that Jews should have a homeland, a safe place for them to be after the Holocaust.

The Holocaust was when a man by the name of Adolf Hitler wanted Germans to be a master race and rule the world. One of the ways to achieve this domination was to "scapegoat" Jews and blame them for everything. To punish them, Hitler put Jews in concentration camps. He killed millions of Jews, including your relatives. Another man in Russia, named Stalin, also thought it was a good idea to kill Jews. He killed part of your great-grandfather's family in what is now known as a pogrom.

Your great-grandparents on your grandmother's side were Holocaust survivors, but I am not sure they believed in God, either. They did believe in being Jewish and they kept the rituals that bind a family and a community together.

So, ask yourself this question: "If God is all good and all powerful, why is there evil in the world?" I am told that a rabbi, after touring the concentration camps of Nazi Germany, said, "I don't understand. Where God was during this time?" As Woody Allen, the filmmaker, observed, "If it turns out there is a God…basically he is an underachiever."

You have to decide for yourself if God created man or man created God. Do things happen randomly or is there an intelligent design to the universe?

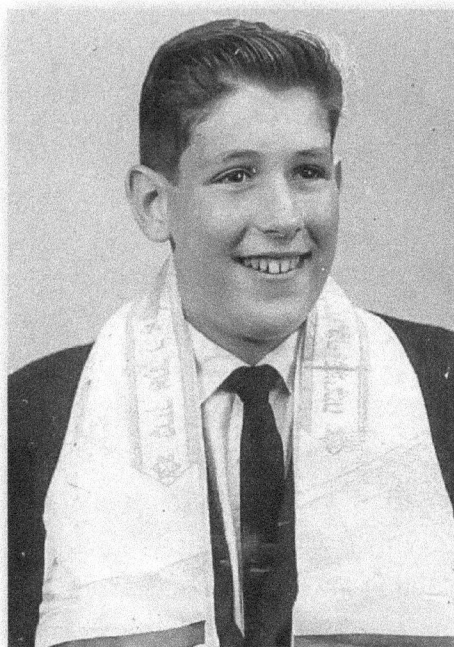

Larry's Bar Mitzvah

At an early point in my life I was very Jewish and very religious, having a Bar Mitzvah in a conservative synagogue. My parents were not religious but they gave me a Bar Mitzvah because it was my life and my choice.

I studied after school in the local Hebrew school for three years and learned to read Hebrew. I was taught to sound out the letters phonetically without having any idea what the words meant. "This skill is important," my Hebrew teacher told me, "because when you are 13, the rabbi will call you up in front of the congregation to read from the holy Torah, and then you will be a man." I studied the phonetics and the chants associated with reading the Torah until I was perfect.

On the day of my Bar Mitzvah two boys went to pulpit and each had a turn at holding the holy Torah. My fear was that the Torah would be too heavy to hold because it contained the holy words which bind all Jews together. The words are read throughout the year and at year's end you start all over again. I did not know what the words said, but surely the silver handles, chains, and emblems of The Scroll symbolized their weighty significance. It would be a humiliation no boy could bear if I were to drop the Torah when it was placed in my custody. Luckily I held the Torah firmly as I circled the congregation to give people an opportunity to kiss their prayer shawls and touch the Torah's cover as a sign of respect for Jewish traditions.

I felt perspiration drip down my forehead until I safely placed the Torah on the pulpit. Victory was mine, and I went on to read my section of the Torah perfectly as the rabbi and cantor smiled with approval. I was so proud that my boyish voice cracked only once during the performance.

Later that afternoon, I had my Bar Mitzvah party at Seniors Restaurant in Sheepshead Bay, Brooklyn, near the New York City housing projects where my mother managed. Needless to say, Seniors was not a kosher restaurant. It was more like a fancy diner with good cheeseburgers, fries, and onion rings. What more could a newly transitioned man ask for? This restaurant was what my family could afford, and I was happy to be the center of the celebration.

Pauline & Sylvia

During the party, I overhead my mother talking to her sister. "That bastard," my mother said to my Aunt Pauline. My mother seldom cursed, so this conversation gained my full attention without either my mother or aunt realizing I was listening. "That rabbi said before the service, 'What are you donating to the temple?' He ask the family of the other Bar Mitzvah boy the same question. They donated far more than I could afford. When the rabbi addressed the congregation after the Torah readings, he heaped all the praise on the other boy and his family and said *bupkis* about Larry."

In my adrenaline rush after the reading, I did not hear the rabbi's comments. How could he have said nothing about me on my proudest day? My reading was perfect, and my rich opponent made plenty of mistakes. This slight bothered me for many weeks and months, but I finally made my peace with it. It seemed that religion, the way it was practiced at this temple, had less to do with spirituality and more to do with raising money. Religion was a business, and like any other business, it was out for itself. If this was so, did I really want to buy what it was selling?

When I was in my twenties, I listened to the comedian George Carlin, who spoke to my feelings on my Bar Mitzvah day. "Religion has actually convinced people that there's an invisible man living in the sky who watches everything you do, every minute of every day. And the invisible man has a special list of ten things he does not want you to do. And if you do any of these ten things, he has a special place, full of fire and smoke and burning and torture and anguish, where he will send you to live and suffer and burn and choke and scream and cry forever and ever 'til the end of time! But He loves you. He loves you, and He needs money! He always needs money! He's all-powerful, all-perfect, all-knowing, and all-wise—somehow just can't handle money!"

Your grandmother Edith Lehrer was raised in a very religious family in Poland and migrated to the United States with her husband William Hoffman after they both survived the Nazi Holocaust. She faced another crisis. Her husband died of a rare, protracted lung cancer, the type that the doctors suspect you get from working in mines in a concentration camp.

Willie was not religious and Edith had felt embarrassed to attend temple without him when he was alive. The few times she did, other woman would ask, "Where is your husband?" and Edith would lie and say, "Over there in the men's section." In her temple, men sat separately from women, which provided Edith a perfect cover story.

However, Edith was now alone. In Edith's loneliness and grief after Willie's death, she turned to her temple. I asked my mother-in-law—who was actually more like a second mother to me—why she'd gone back to her synagogue. She shrugged and said, "You know when they say the prayers in Hebrew? I don't understand them, and being there gives me solace. When they say the prayers in English, and I *do* understand them, and the words don't comfort me."

It was the same for me: I was better off not knowing what the words in my Torah reading meant. The mystery of religious ritual can transport you; the words, not so much.

In time, I became an atheist who does not believe in God, but I still identify as culturally Jewish. I agreed with the atheist Cristopher Hitchens on two basic points. "That which can be asserted without evidence, can be dismissed without evidence," and, "Human decency is not derived from religion. It precedes it."

So, which path will you choose? Should you lead a religious life, be agnostic and not know what to believe, or be an atheist?

It is your life; I cannot tell you what to do. I can only tell you I will love you no matter what you choose. And that is how it should be between a grandfather and grandchild. I will love you without restriction and with all my heart, no matter what you believe.

# On Perspective

———————

PERSPECTIVE IS HOW YOU SEE things. Your point of view can color the way you see. Not everyone sees the same object in the same way. For example, after reading my father's case file, I saw the FBI as dogs who were trained to chase their own tails. They were ordered to do so and never deviated from running in circles, barking at the same information over and over again. Eventually the dogs' spines stretched from all the activity and they gained the ability to see from a new vantage point not only their tails, but also their butts. What could be more illuminating to a national security investigation than a series of dogs with their heads up their asses?

Even after it was handed over to Immigration and Naturalization, memos show that the FBI kept close tabs on my father's case. Their justification was that my father was "Ben," a mysterious espionage agent.

On February 20, 1953, Mathew Math, one of my father's attorneys, asked that the case be reopened and the deportation order suspended based on Section 24 of the Immigration and Naturalization Act. He argued that my father was "a man of good moral character and the father of three children, who needed his advice and guidance, and further that his deportation would effect a hardship on these children." Actually my father had four children.

On June 10, 1953, William Abrams was afforded a new hearing by Immigration and Naturalization Service at Ellis Island. He told the hearing officer I. Millman that "after his break with the Communist Party he was anti-communist as his writings would reflect." The hearing officer asked for him to submit his writing within a month. During this time the FBI was still checking the mail and interviewing people in an attempt to prove my father's secret identity was Ben.

The "good moral character" phrase would become a key to my father's fate. "Under Section 101 (F) of the Immigration Act, no person regarded as a person of good moral character, who, during the period for which good moral character is required, has committed adultery." Hearing Officer Millman continued: "It appears undisputed that the respondent had adulterous relations with his present wife (Sylvia) for some period of time prior to his marriage to his marriage to her in 1945….They actually lived together from 1940 until October 1942….The respondent was divorced from his prior wife (Rose) on July 15 1944….(T)here is no alternative but to order deportation."

What Hearing Officer Millman did not mention is that my father separated from Rose in 1930 and she refused to grant him a divorce. When my mother met my father ten years later, she fell in love and lived with him. She and my father asked Rose for a divorce, which she granted in 1944, so they could get married and have me. In effect, my father was to be deported because he slept with my mother ten years after he separated from Rose. (Oh my God, the shame of it.)

Mr. Chastin, another one of my father's lawyers, argued that Mr. Millman had proceeded upon the erroneous assumption that the period of good moral character should be the ten years immediately preceding the application. In that case, the adultery charges would be relevant. However, Statute Section 244 (A)(5) indicates "the ten year period required is the period following the assumption of status institution the grounds for deportation." In this case, the fact that my father slept with my mother before marriage no longer mattered.

I wonder if any of the prosecutors saw the absurdity in their arguments of guilt by association or adultery. Was it just a game they thought they had to play or did they really believe that my father was unfit to be an American? I guess it is all a matter of perspective.

# On Choice

---

"ONCE, TWICE, THREE, SHOOT," IS what we would say to determine who would go first. If two people wanted the same thing, we would finger-choose. That is when one person calls, "odds," the other, "evens," and on the count of three, each contestant puts out one or two fingers at the same time. If the finger total is two or four, then "evens" wins; one or three, "odds" wins. If you think you might like the outcome, you have to call, "No penny tax," which means no do-overs. If you want to tighten the suspense, you call, "Best two out of three wins."

To have the choice means everything. You can look your opponent in the eye, guess the number of fingers he is intending to "shoot" at the showdown, and, with a calculated but quick reaction, outwit him. The rules of the game are simple and fair; both contestants make sure there is no hesitation in the finger-shoot so the person showing his hand last does not wind up with an unfair advantage.

When I was young, it was fun to choose, fun to win, and even if you lost, the outcome was accepted by all. Sometimes the loser groaned, but that was all part of the game.

I have seen, as you will, the hordes of people who don't know how to choose fairly engage in wars and atrocities as a way to resolve conflict. Your eyes will turn down ever so slightly as you watch the media exploit a senseless death from gun violence, crime, or ethnic genocide to boost ratings without the investigative journalism necessary to probe deeply into the complexities of the conflict. Indeed, you will look at the world and wonder at its horrors and inhumanity. At times you will wonder: Why does it have to be so inhumane? Is there anything we can do to change it? What chances did William and Sylvia have to change the government's web of deportation?

Well, perhaps there is hope. As in the game, you can choose. It is that choice that makes you human.

There will be many people who want to take away your choice. Some may argue there is no such thing as the "free will" that allows a person to choose. Others may argue that even if free will exists, your life is pre-determined and you have no real choice. Life is fated or absurd and there is nothing you can do about it.

So, ask yourself: How do these people know what they know? Even if they are correct, you need to decide what you will choose. Choose safely and wisely, but choose. Your choices are what will define you. Your choices are what make you human.

# On Justice

———

JUSTICE IS BEING IMPARTIAL OR fair or righteous. It is being faithful to truth, fact, or reason. In our society, laws and bureaucratic regulations designed to provide justice often fall short of the ideal.

In my father's case the FBI reduced him to the following description:

**Born:** February 19, 1894
Siaulaui, Kaunas, Russia
(Siavli, Lithuania)

**Height:** 5' 10"

**Weight:** 170 lbs.

**Complexion:** Fair, Dark Beard

**Eyes:** Brown

**Hair:** Black, straight and turning grey

**Occupation:** Journalist, author and lecturer, also wholesaler of watches

**Parents:** Father—Meyer Leiser Abrams deceased
Mother—Rifka Osher (also given as Rebecca Wolfson) deceased

**Marital History:** Married Rose Weiner, February 14, 1918, Brooklyn, divorced July 14, 1944, New York City, son Carl born January 22, 1919: daughter Nina, born May 18, 1921, both New York City

Began living as man and wife with Leah Gessler (deceased) 1927-1936, son Robert, born April 19, 1934, New York City

Began living with Sylvia Berg as man and wife, 1939. Married Sylvia Berg January 5, 1945, Greenwich, Connecticut. A son born of this marriage aged 5 1/2, April 1952

**Arrest Record:** Arrested May 5, 1916, New York City Police Department, grand larceny, dismissed by Grand Jury, May 10, 1916

Arrested May, 190, smoking in subway, paid fine

Arrested INS #A077628, October 17, 1951, as deportable alien recommended for deportation

Bureaucracies like to perpetuate themselves with rules and regulations that provide stability. They reduce people to their records. But is this record correct? Is it just? For example, I was born on August 10, 1946, not in April 1952. In the end, the truth doesn't matter. Bureaucracies can mold the truth to what is expedient. In my father's case, since there were no criminal charges of espionage, the FBI's goal was to disrupt his life and deport him to another country.

Neither my father nor his lawyers had access to the FBI dossier. It shows that after surveying confidential informants who were admittedly familiar with certain phases of Soviet espionage activities and communistic activities in the United States, 14 informants told the FBI that William Abrams, his aliases, and photograph were unknown to them. A 15th informant vaguely recognized him at a German Social Democrats' meeting, and may have met him in the 1930s. (There is a sentiment the Communist Party from the 1930s through the 1950s was composed solely of FBI Confidential Informants. I don't think that is true, but judging from the numbers of confidential informants, the FBI was ever-present in the Communist Party and its affiliates.)

The FBI did not give up on the "Ben" connection. They found a Felix Inslerman who knew the espionage agent Ben and in 1954 the FBI showed a picture of my father for him to identify. Inslerman studied the photograph carefully. He recalled Ben "as having a rounder face and a more pudgy appearance." He also advised that he did not recall Ben as having such distinct wrinkles around the mouth as depicted in the photograph of Abrams. Inslerman added that even if this individual's face were somewhat rounder, he still would not resemble Ben.

There was some attempt to link my father to the famous Alger Hiss case in which Wittaker Chambers, a former Communist Party member, testified in 1948 before the House Un-American Activities Committee that Alger Hiss, a State Department Official, was in fact a communist spy. Hiss denied the charge and later was convicted of perjury. Because my father was not Ben, this "Hail Mary" play flopped badly.

The Immigration and Naturalization Service (INS) ordered my father deported to another country. To execute the order, another country would have to accept him. This process continued for several years. Each week my father would have to report to his parole officer on Ellis Island. Canada refused to accept him. Israel said he was too old. The government wanted to send him back to the Soviet Union, but he fought their suggestion, stating he had no desire to end up in a concentration camp. FBI surveillance continued but not with the same intensity. He decided in 1954 to file a new motion for reconsideration of the INS order that had dismissed his previous appeal from deportation.

On May 15, 1956, his case was considered by the Board of Immigration Appeals, "at which time the order and warrant of deportation were withdrawn and his hearing reopened to afford him an opportunity to appeal for suspension of deportation…."

On October 11, 1956, Louis Totaro, of the Special Inquiry Section of INS stated that, "Because the case was so voluminous it is unlikely any action will be taken before sometime in early 1957."

On January 31, 1957, the FBI reported that the Immigration and Naturalization Service's Office of Special Investigations directed that William Abrams's deportation be suspended. The mood of the country had changed.

On March 9, 1954, Edward R. Murrow, a CBS journalist on *See It Now*, had a conversation with Senator Joe McCarthy and exposed him for the bully he was. McCarthy's "guilt by association" tactics that had led the government into witch-hunting communists in the name of national security were revealed in the media. McCarthy fell from grace, and in the years to follow, the prosecutorial tactics diminished. Still, bureaucracy is slow to react to change. It wasn't until July 7, 1958, through an act of Congress, that my father was granted permanent-resident status in the United States. Finally justice had prevailed. The cloud of persecution was lifted from my family. However, I am not sure my father ever recovered from the justice process.

# On Play

———

PLAY IS ONE OF THE most magical things a child does. Sadly, as they grow older, some people forget how to play. They lose their sense of joy and wonder and become as serious as dried prunes. Adults, if they know what's good for them, should never lose their sense of play.

Meredith At Play

I learned how to play growing up in an apartment building on 80 Winthrop Street in Flatbush, Brooklyn during the late 1950s, early 1960s. I had friends—like Robert Greenberg, Norman Cohen, Allan Lutell, and Stevie Axelrod—who liked to play, too.

We played stickball, hitting a rubber ball, called a Spaldeen, with a mop handle for one or two sewers in the street to score runs for our team.

We played numbers, when we would throw the ball up in the air, let it bounce off of the apartment building's wall, call someone's number, and if that person didn't catch it on the fly during the descent, then he would get a point. If he did catch it, it was his turn to throw the ball into the air and call someone's number. If a person accumulated ten points for not catching the ball when called, then that person had to face "the firing squad." The loser had to bend over and show his butt as the target. Each player would hurl the Spaldeen at the loser's butt as fast as he could from 60 feet. Most times, we missed, but trying to avoid being the target added a sense of danger to the game.

We played Ring-a-levio, when members of one team would try to capture members of the other. If you were touched and captured, you had to go to the home base prison and couldn't be released until another un-caught member of your team touched home base and yelled, "Caw, Caw, Ring-a-levio, 1, 2, 3." At this point, you could scatter and rejoin your team.

My favorite game was Slap Ball because we played it on our secret field. Eighty Winthrop Street was a massive, brick, six-story apartment building with hidden courtyards inside its bowels. We turned one such courtyard into our own Slap Ball Stadium much like Ebbets Field, where our beloved Dodgers played some ten or so blocks away. On three sides our courtyard was surrounded by the brick walls, windows, and fire escapes of the apartment house. On the fourth side there was a rock and cement wall five feet high, with a six-foot, chain-link fence marking the property line of the next lot. It was like we had our own bleachers over the fence where fans could cheer when we made an incredible play.

There were only three exits in our stadium. The one on the right led to a cavernous passage to the street; the one on the left, to another tunnel to the building's rear yard; and the one in the middle, through the basement and to the central courtyard of the building. In fact, there was a fourth exit if one chose to jump the rock wall and scale the fence. The fourth escape was the most difficult because not everyone was agile enough the scale the fence.

We made up rules for our Slap Ball games. There were only three bases: home plate, first, and second. The pitcher would stand at second base and throw a Spaldeen on one bounce with spin, which we called a "fluke." As in baseball, we called each pitch a "ball" or "strike." If you dug your knuckles into the ball and let it roll off your thumb, you would get the ball to bounce right, left, or stop. The "stop," or "change-up," was the most daring pitch. The batter would either look like a fool if he missed timed it or like a hero if he slapped the ball for a hit. If he did make contact, he would have to run to first base before the fielder picked up his grounder and threw him out. If it was a fly ball, if the fielder caught it directly or off the wall, the batter was out. If the fielder missed the carom off the wall, it might lead to extra bases.

Our screams of encouragement to our teammates and our taunts at our opponents' lack of skill bellowed up the walls of the court-yard as if it were a giant echo chamber. We could pretend it was the roar of the crowd when our Dodgers played the dreadful Bronx Giants who were our sworn enemies (except for their center fielder, Willie Mays, "The Say-Hey Kid"). We were partisans and thought Duke Snyder was the better center fielder because he was a great Dodger, like Jackie Robinson, Gil Hodges, Pee Wee Reese, or Sandy Koufax. Objectively, we were wrong. Willie Mays invented the "basket catch," where he would catch a fly ball with his glove waist-high, pointing its web to the sky like a basket. We didn't care because Duke was a Dodger and our home-field territory is what mattered. Loyalty was more important than truth.

It was 1954, and along with my downstairs neighbor Ellen Raast, I came face to face with Jackie Robinson. I was invited onstage to meet him when he spoke at the housing projects my mother managed. He was magnetic both on and off the field. He conquered a relentless persecution by becoming the first Black, or in 1954 terms "Negro," player to break Major League Baseball's color barrier. He faced adversity with dignity. On the field he was a joy to watch as he made third base his territory. He would take extra long leads, daring the opposing pitcher to pick him off. If the pitcher decided to do so, he would dash home, sliding in safely before the tag to the roar of his multicultural Brooklyn fans.

Jackie Robinson & Larry

Like Jackie, we knew how to defend our territory. We knew, when playing Slap Ball, to listen for the sounds of a window creaking open to announce the presence of Ms. Stripp, a cantankerous old lady who lived on the fourth floor and hated children. "You get outta here," she would yell at the top of her feeble lungs as soon as her window was fully open. We knew what would happen next. She would throw a pail full of water, which would splash down like a monsoon. The intensity of the water falling from the fourth floor was so strong that it bounced off the concrete only to impact the cement a second time.

As luck would have it, Ms. Stripp's window was between second base and home plate, and her throwing arm was not strong enough to give players a shower. Our ground rules were intended to keep us both safe and dry. Although Ms. Stripp tried day after day to stymie our play, she missed every time. It seems her life was dedicated to futilely moving a pot of water to the window and hurling it again and again but never hitting her target.

Actually, one time the water did hit Norman Cohen when he was inexplicably between second base and home. He got drenched. The rest of us roared with laughter, which in turn gave Ms. Stripp the motivation to continue her quest.

After many more unsuccessful attempts, Ms. Stripp decided to complain to the super. I did not know it then, but the super was helping the Federal Bureau of Investigation gather information on my father because they suspected him of being a communist. With military precision, the super recruited Henry, the doorman, who came from the south and had always been gentle and kind to the children in the building. Henry would laugh with us and then say, "If you don't behave, I'll slit your gizzard," making a vertical "s" with his hands to show the trajectory of a knife when slitting someone's gizzard. We were unsure of what a gizzard was, but it was something we did not want slit. Not for a moment did we believe Henry would do it. He knew how to play with kids.

The super had a plan to catch us in the act. Mapping out a strategy worthy of a McArthur, one of the great World War II generals, he planned to arrive at the courtyard via the center tunnel while Henry was to simultaneously arrive through the left tunnel. The only flaw was that when we heard them coming, we scattered like water bugs that had just seen a light. We exited through the right tunnel. Excited that we had avoided capture, we waited them out until the coast was clear. Then we resumed our game. In the coming days and weeks, the super tried time and time again to trap us but always left one tunnel free for us to escape.

One day, the day of reckoning, the super decided a three-tunnel approach was needed. He recruited a handyman to block our exit from the third tunnel. On paper, his plan was fool-proof. With all exits blocked, we would be forced to listen to the lecture of our lives and would then be brought in by the scruff of our necks to our parents. We discussed this eventuality and knew we needed a counter strategy. It was like cops-and-robbers, cowboys-and-Indians, hide-and-seek; you had to outwit your opponent to win the game. So when the three-pronged attack commenced, we were ready.

We had secretly cut a hole in the chain-link fence over the five-foot rock wall. When we heard them coming, we gained a quick foothold on the wall, catapulted to the top, and even the slower climbers were able to quickly slide through. As we headed to the safety of the next building's yard, which was not visible from our pursuers' vantage point, we could hear curses emanating from our Slap Ball Stadium. Our victory was sweet, but like MacArthur, we knew the super would return. It was all part of the glorious game that we loved to play.

If you would ask me what I learned in school during this time that would guide me later in life, I would not be able to tell you. If you asked me what I learned in play, the answer would be a whole lot.

# On Irony

———◆———

THE OXFORD ENGLISH DICTIONARY DEFINES irony as something that has a different or opposite result from what is expected. So if someone tells you that have to work the whole weekend, an ironic response would be, "How nice." Often in life, ironies crop up when you least expect them. I experienced one such irony when I was a social studies teacher in the late 1970s and early 1980s at John Dewey High School in the Gravesend section of Brooklyn.

The school had been created in 1969 by a group of high school principals who were charged with designing a structure that would educate students better than the traditional assembly-line high school did. They created a school with five cycles per year instead of two semesters. Teachers worked eight hours a day, not the standard six hours and twenty minutes, and much of that time was channeled into resource centers, which were mini-libraries in each subject area scattered around the school, where students could get the individual attention needed to "master" a subject. Instead of numerical grades, there were the following levels: mastery with excellence, mastery, mastery with condition, and no credit. As in college, students had "free time" in their daily programs in which they could choose to go to a resource center, attend co-curricular activity, or just hang out. Students had the option of completing a course by Dewey Independent Study Kit (DISK), for which they were given specific individual lessons to complete and a mentor-teacher to help them through the process.

By the mid-'70s, I had left Sheepshead Bay High School and was helping to develop The Executive High School Internship Program, which was a mentoring program replacing a semester of either the junior or senior year. A "school without walls" concept was interesting to me, but in the end I wasn't doing the teaching, which I loved, but rather structuring experiences so some executives in the public or private sector could provide educational experiences for the students I had recruited. I had friends at John Dewey High School, and they said it had attracted one of the best teaching staffs. I missed teaching and figured here was a place to hone my skills, so I applied for a job and was hired as a social studies teacher.

Learning from my peers, I quickly improved my craft. In the 1980s I was teaching a five-cycle course called "The American Dream" which was a combination of American history and literature used to augment the history. The course was designed to keep students actively engaged in the learning. I team-taught the class with my good friend Paul Weiss.

In the colonial period, we had students read and act out Arthur Miller's *The Crucible* as a study in the pressures to conform and engage in witch-hunts that appear throughout American history.

An enemy is needed to stir up a sense of patriotism. Paul and I had a joyous time teaching together. One student brought in a "poppet" (puppet) which had red hair and was modeled on Mr. Weiss. There is a scene in *The Crucible* where the townsfolk of Salem believe these "poppets" are possessed.

Now, the walls between our classrooms were moveable and not soundproof. Paul and I conspired that five minutes before the end of the period, I would go into a rant about how silly people were to believe a voodoo doll in a human image could control someone. Two minutes before the period ended, I would prove my point and shove a sharp pin into the doll's heart. As I did, it was Paul's timed cued to double over in pain and scream at the top of his lungs. When we pulled this stunt for real, the students in both classes went berserk, the bell rang, and the class was dismissed with students giggling from excitement as only high school students can. Paul and I met up after class laughing about our intricate prank and describing the facial expressions of each of the students we knew so well. (Ironically, years later, Paul died at a much too young age from a heart attack after one of his "power walks.")

In the course, Paul and I did various simulations that were extended role plays to give the students a deeper insight into a particular time in history. For example, we simulated The Constitutional Convention, with students acting as delegates with different interests who had to draft founding document. We had The North and The South decide who was responsible for the Civil War by examining and cross-examining historical witnesses. When we got to the 1950s, we had investigators from a model House Un-American

Activities Committee accuse and depose various historical suspected communists to see if they could get them to admit their affiliation and incriminate others.

I am not quite sure whose idea it was, but at the end of our McCarthy simulation, we would send out letters asking people with knowledge of the era to have a Q-and-A session with our classes. One year, Roy Cohn accepted. Though you may not know his name, Roy Cohn was a very big deal. He was a member of the U.S. Justice Department team that prosecuted Julius and Ethyl Rosenberg for espionage in stealing atomic secrets from "The Manhattan Project." J. Edgar Hoover recommended Roy Cohn to Senator McCarthy, who hired him as chief counsel. The other candidate was Robert Kennedy, but it is alleged that McCarthy chose to use Cohn's Jewish background to shield him from being labeled an anti-Semite. Cohn was especially active in the Second Red Scare, investigating communist activity in the United States.

Paul Weiss and I prepared our class to think about relevant questions they could ask Mr. Cohn. They discussed some ideas and waited impatiently for Mr. Cohn's visit. Roy Cohn arrived promptly, his chauffeur driving his Rolls Royce into John Dewey's parking lot. I have no way to substantiate this observation, but I am sure that his car was the first Rolls Royce ever parked in the John Dewey lot.

As I greeted Roy Cohn, I saw that he was impeccably dressed and had short-cropped hair and steel blue eyes that, when you looked into them, penetrated you. I thought I was seeing into his soul or perhaps just looking into a void which could move in any direction. I told him it was nice of him to take the time to speak with our students, hiding all my emotions from my youth. In New York City, social studies teachers are trained not to take any political position, but to let students figure things out for themselves in a process known as "values clarification." Simply put, you are a teacher, not a preacher.

Roy Cohn addressed the class and, to his credit, answered their questions for an hour. He answered each respectfully, and our students responded with follow-up questions just as respectfully. Many of the questions were challenging but based on historical facts.

When the session was completed, he told me that he speaks at many college campuses where the students ask him questions about the McCarthy era and his role in it. Today he thought the level, depth, and specificity from our students surpassed by leaps and bounds the type of questions he received on college campuses. I thanked him for his generosity in giving his time to speak to the students and walked him and his chauffeur back to the car. I glanced quickly to make sure the wheels were still on the Rolls. He thanked me for an interesting afternoon, said good-bye, and drove away.

Approximately a week later I received a copy of a letter from Roy Cohn, addressed to the Chancellor of New York City Schools, commending Mr. Weiss and me for the job we are doing with our students. I read the letter three times. I wondered what my father would think. Would he appreciate the irony?

Roy Cohn died on August 2, 1986 from complications from AIDS Michael Kruse in *Politico Magazine* (April 8, 2016) links Roy Cohn to Donald Trump in the 13-year period before Cohn's death. The author accuses Cohn of red-baiting, demagoguery, fear-mongering, and character assassination. Kruse also claims: "Cohn was one of the most powerful influences and helpful contacts in Trump's life." Cohn's "say anything, win-at-all-costs style" became embedded Trump's business deals and in "the belligerent public persona visible in Trump's presidential campaign."

The article is just one man's opinion. However, how ironic it is that the author thinks Trump is another incarnation of Cohn. Cohn's style worked and served him well. Unfortunately the same cannot be said for my father and all the others who had their lives put on hold during McCarthy's reign.

# On Bullying

———◆———

PECKING ORDERS EXIST NOT BECAUSE chickens have beaks; they exist to structure social interactions. Who will be the groomer and who will be groomed is the very essence of social behavior. It gives us not only neatness, but also a way of understanding the world.

It was in the early 1960s on the streets of Flatbush, Brooklyn. Teens attending Erasmus Hall High School were listening to Buddy Holly and the Comets, Elvis, the Beach Boys, and of course The Beatles. Hair styles were slicked back in a D.A. (duck's ass) for boys and a pageboy flip for girls. We roamed the streets with friends, looking for the next adventure, and tried to be cool. When a Corvette convertible drove by us in the street, all heads would turn in unison. We were like chickens who got a glimpse of the status we could achieve given the right circumstances.

Rather than see the wonder of being young and in a group, there were those who believed they had to elevate their status through violence. Peter Raisen was one such kid. He was a bully. He dressed in one of those muscle tee shirts with straps instead of sleeves to show off his biceps. His hair was properly greased and his eyes a deep brown that revealed not a flicker of inner intelligence. His way to the top was to stomp people into submission. This night, he chose me as his next victim.

I was walking down Lenox Road with my friends when I heard his voice in back of me calling me out. "Hey, you, I've been looking for you." He was accompanied by six of his cohorts who outflanked us in a well-choreographed pincer movement. My friends stopped in their tracks with me in the middle. Peter thrust his hands into my chest and said, "I'm coming for you." Peter was slightly taller than I was and somewhat heavier. He had a reputation for liking to pick on kids he thought he could intimidate in order to increase his "street cred."

The sense of the looming fight was in the air and other unattached boys gathered to see the spectacle. I was later told there were members of the Egyptian Lords, a street gang, in the gathering crowd. Its leader Waco Simmons was known for stabbing people with a stiletto. His first name alone sounded like it belonged to someone crazy. One didn't mess with Waco Simmons.

At first I froze as my eyes met Peter's. Unless I wanted to be a chicken for the rest of my life, there was no way out but to fight back. "I'll fight you," I responded to his chest shove, "But I want a fair, one-on-one fight." Somehow it was decided that we should move off the street into a back alley so the cops wouldn't see us. The alley led to a courtyard. I found myself surrounded by a crowd of 20 or so teenagers waiting for the first drop of blood. Peter threw a roundhouse right at me and I blocked it.

The crowd roared. I jabbed at his head with my right, thinking it would keep him off balance until I could think of what to do. This strategy was somewhat counterintuitive and it annoyed Peter. I was probing the least vulnerable part of his body. He lunged at me and his full 190 pounds came up to my chest in a bear hug. Surprised, I wriggled downward and Peter wrapped his meaty arm around my head and twisted my neck upward. At this point I heard the grunts from the crowd and Peter's deep, laborious breathes, punctuated by the smell of his oozing sweat, grinding me into submission. His fingers were placed over my mouth, clenching my jaw.

If I was going to survive, I had to act now. I don't quite know how it happened, but my teeth found Peter's pointer finger and I clenched down on it as hard as I could. He released the headlock and cried out in pain. "If you don't stop biting my finger, I am going the kick the crap out of you," he screamed at the top of his lungs. The crowd went silent. I knew if I released his finger, he would try to beat the crap out of me, so I didn't let go for what must have been an eternity. Sniveling, he begged for mercy and finally I relented. After he regained his composure, he threw a few more punches. He landed some, I landed some, but it was evident that the fight was out of him. His finger throbbing; he retreated. The onlookers dispersed, and I was left with my friends for a post-fight analysis.

"How did you think to do that?" my friend Bruce said. I gave him a dazed look. He continued, "Do you know one of the Egyptian Lords was in the crowd and he had a knife? I told him to put it away and let you have a fair fight. In the end you had that Raisen f*** crying like a baby." Peter Raisen never bothered me again.

Days, weeks, and even decades later, I think about that fight. I had no way out and could have been killed in that back courtyard on Lenox Road. How stupid, yet "dem's da rules of the game when you grow up in Brooklyn." I had to use force to protect myself or else I would have been labeled a coward, demoted in the pecking order, and, worst of all, ashamed of myself.

Years later, when I had the opportunity to design my own public school in Brooklyn, I saw how children, if not given proper structure, can become like chickens in a barnyard. They "rank" on each other verbally to establish dominance. Sooner or later the verbal abuse leads to fighting and physical abuse, which is often tolerated as part of the normal school day.

As principal, I told my students and teachers I wanted this school to be a kinder and gentler place. I wanted it to be a place where people could feel safe so learning could happen. I invested a great deal of staff development money in conflict resolution programs so students would know how to use words to describe their feelings and mediate possible conflicts. I wanted them to respect each other's differences and never "rank" on each other. Diversity is a strength that can teach us the right way to problem solve. It is not a weakness to be exploited by a bully.

Other principals with whom I've worked, especially on the high school and middle school levels, do not invest time in developing the affective side of their students' education. They prefer the cognitive side, to increase their academic knowledge. I think about these principals as I see the violence erupting in our school system.

I wonder: What ever happened to Peter Raisen? Did he ever finish high school, go to college, and make something out of his life? Or is he still stuck as a teenager, a slave to his hostility, unable to make the collaborative connections necessary for success? Did he become an outsider, isolated, sullen, and alone, craving attention and instilling fear in others? Or did he master the communications systems via cell phone texts and emails, writing the kinds of messages that bully so many vulnerable teenagers today? Did he invent "sexting," which teenagers often use to experiment with flirting—only to then be led down a path of humiliation?

When I take a step back and look at the bullying going on in our world, I pause for a moment and wonder whether Peter Raisen won our fight after all.

The thing about bullies is that they have many incarnations and different levels of sophistication. If you strip away the veneer, is Peter Raisen really so different from J. Edgar Hoover, Senator Joe McCarthy, Roy Cohen, Donald Trump, Bashar al-Assad of Syria, or Kim Jong-un of North Korea? The choice is to support or deny people's human rights. Bullies create an "enemy" to amass their own power and justify their indecent actions. They subscribe to the big lie that their power can create truth. They believe fear is more effective than love.

My mother and father were just bit players on the human stage; however, they became branded by the fear of communism. Though they didn't have the notoriety the press assigned to big "red herrings" like Alger Hiss, the government's whispering campaign effectively disrupted their lives for many years. To confront this level of injustice is not as simple as walking into a back alley. It is a choice humane people around the world must make every day, in vastly different situations, if human rights are to survive.

# On Safety

—

MY MOTHER SYLVIA WAS AN honest and most remarkable woman. As my mother, she would do everything in her power to protect me and keep me safe.

Sylvia was born on September 10, 1912 to Meyer Berg and Marion Lamb. The Lamb family circle's claim to fame was that it produced Norman Lamb, who was a noted conservative rabbi and head of Yeshiva University. Sylvia had two sisters, Betty Brooke and Pauline Attkiss, and a brother, Sam Berg. At one time her parents ran a restaurant in Manhattan and she helped wait the tables. She graduated with a Bachelor of Arts degree from Hunter College in 1935, majoring in political science and history. From 1930 to 1934, she worked for a Park Avenue plastic surgeon, whom she described as a nasty man. When he fired her without cause, she protested and said, "Why did you hire me in the first place?" He responded, "I wanted to show my patients what the 'before' looked like."

In 1935, she was an administrator for a remedial reading program, and in 1939, an adult education instructor teaching English to the foreign-born. In 1940, she was an investigator for the Department of Welfare. After that, she joined the New York City Housing Authority with the idealism that the project system would lift people out of poverty.

She stayed single until she married my father in 1945. She became the breadwinner in the family, which was unusual in the 1950s, when suburban housewives in aprons were the norm. She was bright, independent, and rose to the position of manager for the New York City Housing Authority.

On November 24, 1959, an internal FBI report investigating her for perjury described her as follows:

**Age:** 46-47

**Race:** White

**Sex:** Female

**Height:** 5' 5"

**Weight:** 135 pounds

**Hair:** Brown

**Eyes:** Brown

**Residence:** 80 Winthrop Street, Brooklyn, N.Y.

**Occupation:** Housing Manager, Sheepshead Bay and Nostrand Housing Project, 2955 Avenue W, Brooklyn, N.Y.

Other documents described her as having a "young appearance, oval face, sharp piercing eyes (and) well dressed." My mother would have laughed because she didn't consider herself well-dressed. What does that say about the fashion sense of the FBI agent who wrote the document?

As investigations into my father waned, the FBI and Justice Department investigated my mother. This continued through 1959. In the early 1940s, my mother had been active in union work. It is possible that the Communist Party may have acquired knowledge of her and used her name. On February 27, 1956, my mother testified in front of a subcommittee reporting to the House Un-American Activities Committee that she "denied Communist Party membership; denied attendance at closed meetings of the Communist Party; and stated that nobody had approached her concerning the Communist Party or has, (as far as) she knows any Communist Party members in regard to her work in the New York City Housing Authority." An FBI inter-view on November 26, 1956 states it was "shocking to her to be confronted with information linking her name in any way with a subversive organization, pointing out that she always felt she had fully expressed to others her preferred belief in the democratic form of government which exists in this country. The subject stated she is opposed, without reservation, to the Communist Party or any organization which would seek to overthrow the government by force or violence."

Through the Freedom of Information Act, I secured 170 pages of the 176 pages that the FBI has on file about my mother. The file started on January 21, 1955 was an offshoot of my father's investigation. It contained descriptions of my father driving my mother to work in the morning in our blue DeSoto with the license plate number 9K 39-95 and then returning alone to the apartment. Since my father could not find work due to his investigation, the FBI agent reports that my father also picked my mother up from work and then returned home to the apartment at about 5:30 P.M. Over the many days of surveillance, there was a deviation in the pattern that could be noted as suspicious: As reported to the FBI Director, sometimes my mother took the DeSoto and drove herself to work.

There were many photographic surveillance pictures of my mother shown to the FBI confidential informants to see if they could identify her as an active member of the Communist Party. There was interview after interview in New York City and in other cities. Except for two people, no one claimed to be able to give any information regarding her relationship to the Communist Party.

The FBI files show a lot of smoke but little evidence to support my mother was a communist. They looked through the communications of Federal Judge Harold B. Medina at the U.S Court House on Foley Squire in New York City. People, including my mother, signed petitions directed to the judge to save Julius and Ethyl Rosenberg. The Rosenbergs were convicted of espionage and many Jews felt it was anti-Semitism rearing its ugly head even though Roy Cohn was part of the prosecution team. (It is reported that Cohn prided himself on his behind-the-scenes negotiations to secure the death penalty for the Rosenbergs.) My mother also went to several rallies to save the Rosenbergs. In the most controversial espionage case of the Cold War, the Rosenbergs were electrocuted in in June 19, 1953. The FBI had my mother's name on a petition, which proved, in their minds, that she was a red sympathizer.

On December 20, 1954, an informant told the FBI agent that Sylvia Berg told him in 1946 that "she was a member of the Communist Party." He said that Berg introduced him to her husband and he was a member of the Communist Party. The informant, who is a self-identified member of the Communist Party, added that he "does not recall seeing her at any Communist Party meetings."

In a report on November 28, 1955 regarding the investigation into whether my mother committed perjury when she denied she was a communist to the House Un-American Activities Committee, an informant said my mother may have been a member of the Communist Party for "unknown dates." The report states "this information was merely opinion." The informant could furnish no definite information…." He was dropped as an informant in 1955 "on the premise that he would eventually embarrass the Bureau as he was apparently concentrating on every effort to regain his NY Civil Service job, from which he had been dropped from absenteeism."

As a result of my mother's interview in 1956, the FBI concluded her "activities do not to warrant her inclusion on the Security Index."

By January 1957—aside from the "adultery charges" leveled against my father for living in sin with my mother—the investigations into both of them were winding down. Then on February 26, 1957, *The New York Daily News* dropped a bombshell. It ran an article on page three entitled "Tag 5 Project Mgrs. as Red" The article stated that at least five project managers from the New York Housing Authority had been identified as communists by witnesses. Thirteen managers in total were mentioned, and my mother's name was on the list. The Director of the FBI, Mr. Hoover, wanted to know what actions the New York Office was contemplating. Since my mother denied under oath that she ever was a communist, the FBI decided to pursue perjury charges with the Justice Department.

On April 11, 1957, the FBI had called in all thirteen suspects mentioned in *The Daily News* article "Communist Infiltration of the New York City Housing Authority." The FBI interviewed Sylvia Berg (Abrams) and was "unable to obtain specific information… as to the identities of the five project managers." On February 12, 1959, the FBI decided to resurrect the statement of the initial informant who was a self-admitted communist. He was the one who named my mother as a communist based on a 1946 conversation but never saw her at any meetings. As a result, she was pursued by government surveillance from 1954 through 1960. It was the hope that this informant's statement would add credence to the perjury charges.

The Department of Justice interviewed my mother on November 17, 1959 in Brooklyn. At the interview, she "denies present or past membership in the Communist Party; and that she was (n)ever approached by anyone to join the Communist Party or to transfer membership within the Communist Party."

In a memo dated December 14, 1959, Assistant Attorney General J. Walter Yeagley informed the FBI Director the "investigation has not developed any admissible evidence concerning the possible perjury violation. No further investigation is contemplated at this time." On March 9, 1960 the case was closed—a case in which one statement made in 1946 by an eventually discredited confidential informant, and never corroborated, had led to an investigation spanning years.

My mother and father were now safe. As Benjamin Franklin, a founding father of our American democracy, observed in his memoirs, "They who can give up essential liberty to obtain a little temporary safety deserve neither liberty nor safety." My parents had the courage to stay the course. In doing so they kept me truly safe in a world littered with bullies. Their silent teachings molded how I chose to live my life.

LESSON 14

# On Learning

——◆——

I NEVER LIKED HIGH SCHOOL much. I had bigger dreams and just wasn't interested in what many teachers were teaching. Luckily I was in the "honors track," as they called it, where if you earned a grade less than 85, you were considered a failure. So I continued my daily schedule, similar to the other 4,000 students attending Erasmus Hall High School on double session, wanting to be recognized for individual achievements but in the end remaining a product of an educational assembly line.

Erasmus, located in a gothic fortress on Flatbush Avenue, enveloped a whole city block from Flatbush to Bedford Avenues and from Church Avenue to Snyder Avenues. Inside was a courtyard with a green campus. There stood the original Dutch schoolhouse and in front of it a bronze statue of Desi (Desiderius Erasmus) posed reading a book. The open book was above even the tallest student's head. It was said that if you had a test coming up and you managed to throw a coin so high it landed in the book, you would do well on your exam. The exams—usually multiple choice, because those were easy to grade—led teachers to discover who was to be ranked as the most successful learners. The school could point to famous alumni as evidence to perpetuate the myth of the success. They included Barbara Streisand, Neil Diamond, Mae West, Lainie Kazan, and Mickey Spillane—just to name a few.

I tolerated high school but never understood the importance of what I was learning other than that it would be on a State test and that I needed to earn a Regents' Scholarship by doing well on these exams. I did manage to earn a Regents' Scholarship but really did not understand why I was learning. It was rote, and the more you spit back, the better you did. If you did not conform to the assembly-line practice then you would be placed in a lower track, such as "secretarial" or the dreaded "general" diploma. The counseling system divided students into the smarties, the not-as-smarties, and the dummies, with the theory that the bottom two tracks would aspire to the upper levels; however, once you were tracked, you made friends and were more likely to remain in your designated niche.

Here is an illustration of how the system worked: Academic or Regents track students, of which I was one, had to take shop class to perfect their skills. I had the raspy-throated Mr. Erdin in woodworking shop, and our goal for the quarter was to complete a wooden duck which would float, be painted, and serve as a decoy for the masses of duck hunters in Brooklyn. I loved my duck and carefully used a jigsaw to carve its base and body from the templates. Eventually we would countersink a screw through the base and attach the body to it at a right angle.

I wanted the body of my duck to be unique and not have the perfectly flowing back hump designed by the template. I sanded my duck carefully until the slope on its humped back was irregular but as smooth as my tender brushings with sandpaper could make it. I then painted it black, teal, and yellow, the perfect colors for my duck. The next day, when I arrived in Woodshop, Mr. Erdin handed me my duck with raw scars of freshly grated wood over the hump on its back. He had used a harsh rasp to reshape my duck's back hump into something he thought would fit his model of what a duck should be. My carefully brushed paint job had been desecrated by Mr. Erdin's corrections.

"That's better," he said handing me my deformed duck in a voice that reminded me of the rasp which defiled my creation. "Are you f***ing 'quackers,'" I wanted to yell, but my tongue froze in time and I said nothing. I went on to sand the groove marks he left to smooth out and repaint my duck's bruised back. My duck was destined to look like all the other ducks, and there was little I could do to change its fate.

About 35 years later, I had the rare opportunity to create and design my own school. One reason I went into teaching was that I thought anyone could do it better than what I experienced at Erasmus Hall. In Erasmus, I was told what I had to learn and preferred to hang out in Spinelli's pool room or Leader Lanes Bowling Alley, or to watch *Dr. No*, the first James Bond film, at the RKO Kenmore movie theater on Church Avenue. Teachers rarely checked the cutting sheets, and I knew how to play the system. Once I was in college and graduate school, there were no cutting sheets. I could pick classes I wanted to learn and found learning fun. I took ownership of my education.

In the school I founded, we would no longer follow the traditional New York State Regents Diploma where learning curricula are controlled by lobby groups who decide what learnings from each subject area are important. Traditionalists question whether students can learn without multiple choice tests driving the instruction. Traditionalists are comfortable with knowledge that is an inch deep and a mile wide, as tested by the State. Students' understanding of complex issues must have considerably more depth than an inch if our future generations are to have a future.

By contrast, with my teachers, I would create a system whereby students could graduate by doing projects in a portfolio to show their mile-deep knowledge of a specific subject area. The students along with the teacher would be able to evaluate and assess whether the project was good enough to meet standards. The teacher might model excellence in a mini-lesson so that the students, using their creativity, could create a work that met or exceeded standards.

Teachers were not allowed to lecture. Instead, they had to coach students to succeed. Students had to be active participants in the classroom. Students often worked in heterogeneous groups to teach each other the best way of completing a task. Class size was reduced to about half of what it would have been in a typical large, New York City factory school. Rather than having 40 minute periods, class periods were extended to 80 and 120 minutes in the schedule to give students time to complete their projects before moving onto the next subject. Many teachers team-taught to integrate curricula and to focus students on in-depth learning.

Teachers served as advisors who had to look after students, shepherding them from when they first entered the school through graduation. They were concerned about who the students were and used their relationships to raise their expectations. The school's mission of understanding ourselves, the world, and how to make change dealt with both the affective and cognitive learnings necessary for success.

To this day, I am very proud of the good work the teachers and students did in the school. Small schools can be powerful change agents if structured properly. In the end, I created the antithesis of Erasmus Hall High School. I gave my students the opportunity to own their educations unlike what I experienced in high school.

Countries like Finland have developed some of the best public educational systems using active learning and problem-solving techniques. In the United States, many school systems feel it is necessary to burden students with rote homework and lessons to pass standardized examinations. In Finland, educators know this approach is counter-productive. Total school time is less than it is in the United States and homework is not given simply to fill students' days up with chores.

Children need to play, be creative, and interact with other children in their downtime. They need to learn to be happy and that a community cares about them. They need their society to value the "huggle," which is the act of hugging, cuddling, and snuggling all in one go. It is the warm, fuzzy time you spend with your family and friends. It allows you to feel safe and grow as a person all at once. It is a key to happiness. Americans need to devote time to mastering the art of the "huggle." Our lagging public education system would certainly improve if we did.

In Finland, childhood is a time to treasure creativity and let each pupil develop as an individual who can take ownership of what they learn and how they can demonstrate their achievements. Too often, in calling for higher uniform standards, State education officials blot out any joy in learning. It is a sad fact that most Americans do not know how to truly educate students. Our public school system is one of the worst in the industrialized world. And as much as we search, we won't find the truth or the solution on a multiple choice examination.

# On Judgment

SOMETIMES THE BEST JUDGMENT IS to make no judgment at all. My mother, who was a very perceptive woman, regularly ended her stories with the phrase "if you like that sort of thing." Michael bought his wife Carol a large diamond ring, which is very nice, if you like that sort of thing. The phrase left the judgment open as to whether or not the diamond ring was a good thing. Beauty is in the eye of the beholder, and being able to see an issue from all sides opens your perspective. What she did well was to accept all types of people without judgment. She just dealt with them as people, with no preconceived notions. The tenants in her project, who were mostly minority and poor, learned to trust her. She knew how to listen.

My mother had the courage to pursue what was right. The New York City Housing Authority had a glass ceiling for female managers and they only promoted men to higher positions like District Chief. She joined with other female managers and sued the housing authority for equitable treatment. This suit took courage since women were treated as second-class workers in the 1950s and '60s. The women managers won the case, and in time the Housing

Authority promoted my mother to District Chief. Her judgment to pursue her interest in spite of the male-oriented status quo is to be admired.

As a child of the Great Depression in the 1930s, my mother was what you would call "frugal" regarding what she spent on herself and her wardrobe. She used the money she had to help others. Education was one of her core values, and she made sure I had the money to go to college and graduate school. I never had to worry about student loans. She also gave my brother Bob, her step-son, money to attend New York Law School when he was in his fifties. He became a lawyer, which was a boost from the insurance and private investigation work he had been doing. She also lent money to friends and family when they were in need. When I questioned her about some of her loans, she simply shrugged and said, "It is only money. What else is it good for?" She taught me that parents and grandparents need to be responsible and open up opportunities for their offspring. It is an obligation that should never be denied.

After my father died at the age of 74, my mother eventually moved to 400 Rugby Road in the Ditmas Park West section of Brooklyn, one-and-a-half blocks from my old Victorian house at 522 Rugby Road. My mother and my wife Sandy's parents had helped us with the down payment. I loved having her close by, but she was not an intrusive mother. She had her life and network of friends as well as a Teamster's Union local in Manhattan where she took life-long learning classes in Italian. She had an awful ear for language but did make a liaison with a gentleman named Isadoro, with whom she could practice Italian, among other things. When he wanted to get married, my mother told him, "My son will never allow it." When she told me the story, I replied, "Mom, I never said any such thing." She responded, "I know, but the only thing he will accept is my family doesn't want it. He is Italian, you know," she said with a laugh.

At this stage in her life, she wanted her independence. Eventually she moved to a 75 Henry Street in Brooklyn Heights. Her one-bedroom apartment had a view of the harbor and the Statue of Liberty. She was happy with her view of heaven outside her living room and bedroom windows. On her terrace she had a small table and two outdoor chairs, one for her and one for God.

No matter how busy I was, I tried to see her once a week. She had awful cooking skills. One of the reasons I became a good cook is that I needed to survive her lunches and dinners. (She did make excellent bacon-and-egg breakfasts, and her French toast was pretty good, too.) To be safe, we always had dinner at our favorite restaurant, Noodle Pudding, where we discussed the week's events. The owner of the restaurant, Tony, got to know us well. Sandy and Meredith would join us for our weekly meetings. (When Meredith got engaged, we first met her fiancé's parents at Tony's restaurant. It has been a family gathering place for years.) Our conversations were always open and honest, and we could tell each other anything and the other person would listen without judgment. When my mother died on November 20, 2000, at the age of 88, the person I had the most difficult time telling was Tony.

Before she died, she worried about Meredith. She loved her and wanted to make sure she had a nest egg. My mother's apartment at 75 Henry Street was "going public," which meant that when the conversion was complete, people would own their own apartments and could sell them on the open market. The market price of the apartment would skyrocket. My mother established Meredith's name on the lease enabling her to inherit the apartment and be entitled to its equity. In this, case she made an excellent judgment.

Deciding when to follow your judgment and when to let things slide is a balancing act. My mother had very good balance. I learned her style by thinking before I advocate a particular path. In life, I should not be surprised by the people who don't think before they act, but in reality, I constantly am. Like my mother, I need to understand diverse points of view before I react to them.

# On Work

———————

EVERY MORNING IN MARCH, AT around 8:45 A.M., I walk downhill on Mesones, one of the many cobblestone streets in San Miguel de Allende, a colonial Mexican town several hours north of Mexico City. I watch people as they line up to board the old, cranky public buses that transport them to work each weekday. I study their faces to see if there is any hint of joy buried within their day, much as I do when I ride the subways in New York during rush hour. Different church bells melodiously chime in the background every 15 minutes, filling the air with a spirituality that is missing from the workers' expressions.

I watch my step as I proceed down the cobblestones. Though these streets have a colonial charm, it is easy to twist an ankle and fall if you don't pay attention. A fall could be considered an apt price to pay to walk among such architectural beauty. Only the teenaged girls dare to wear high heels to negotiate the cobblestones—and only if they have a date, party, or wedding to attend where they must look like the magazine image. For everyone else, flats become the great equalizer.

I pass the public park with its laurel trees' leaves shaped into tight rectangles which provide shade for the benches below. The topiary is so tight it prevents most birds from nesting in the trees, thus saving the people who sit on the benches below the indignity of experiencing bird poop landing on them.

Meat Delivery Man

Each morning, parked in the same position, is the white meat delivery truck with long clear plastic slits covering the rear cargo entrance. Each morning, a man weighing about 140 pounds and wearing a white cotton butcher's coat stares into the truck. He waits for another man in a similar coat but with blood stains from the racks of meat inside splattered over it in patterns akin to a

Jackson Pollock drip painting. Each slab of meat must easily be 80 to 100 pounds.

The second man slings a half of a cow across his back and slowly dismounts the truck. The first man assists him but is careful not to let any residual blood stain his coat. The second man, hunched over from the weight of his load proceeds 100 feet up the street and delivers the carcass to a butcher shop. The men then return to the truck and drive off, presumably to deliver the remaining racks of meat hanging in the back to different butcher shops around the city.

After watching this same delivery routine for several days, I asked myself, "Are these workers happy? And, if so, is the first worker with the clean coat happier than the second worker with the blood stained coat?"

To be happy, Sigmund Freud said, human beings have to do two things well: love and work. We will cover love in another chapter. Now it is time for work.

Albert Camus wrote about the myth of Sisyphus, a Greek man who tried to escape the underworld. As punishment, the gods condemned him to push a heavy stone uphill. He toiled and toiled at this task, and when he finally push the stone to the top of the hill, the stone under its own weight rolled back to the bottom. Sisyphus watched the stone descend. With each downward roll it picked up speed only to settle at the hill's base, right where it had started.

When Sisyphus saw the stone rolling downward, do you think he was happy? Or was he disappointed that he had to start the same task over, and do it over and over again?

Work can either condemn you, like it condemned Sisyphus, or help you make something special of your life. Sisyphus's work had no meaning, yet he was forced to toil at a task he never could complete. No matter how long he tried, he could never get a sense of satisfaction that he accomplished something important.

Too many people treat work as something they have to do. They ride the subways or public buses with blank stares on their faces, going to jobs they have to do. They get caught up in a routine that is meaningless. In the end, it robs them of their worth.

To avoid this pitfall, it is imperative that you find a career for which you have a passion. Other than a true love, this decision is one of the most important decisions you will make. It will mold you in ways you can't imagine. It has to be something that is economically viable so you can support yourself and be truly independent. Some people follow their passions only to find out they cannot make a living and become disgruntled. Others only follow the money, figuring that the more they make, the happier they will be. Unfortunately, they do not understand that there are riches money can't buy. They forget the passion that makes work exciting and replace creativity with dollar signs. To be happy in your career choice, you will have to find a balance between the two extremes.

I became a teacher because I love the art of teaching. For me, there was no better way to spend my professional life. As a teacher, I had the money I needed to be creative and I could enjoy what I did each day, knowing I was giving people insights about learning that they did not have when they first stepped into my classroom. I loved my job, and unbeknownst to me, my love for it would help me become an assistant principal and finally a principal who founded his own school designed to engage students in their learning.

My daughter, your mother, never wanted to be a teacher. After graduating college, she went to work for a Chinese company on the 101$^{st}$ floor of the World Trade Center. She helped organize a reception for the mayor of Beijing and discovered she liked event planning. She had a passion for it and parlayed it into a career. Now she is the Vice President of a high-end corporate events company whose clients are very prestigious businesses. She followed her heart and her head and became independent and creative within the corporate world. She left the World Trade Center approximately five years before it was destroyed by terrorists. (Terrorists see themselves as pushing a stone up a hill in the name of justice. Like Sisyphus, they are condemned, prisoners of their actions. Timing in life is random. The good news is that you often have the power to control your own choices. Sometimes, you will be conscious of that power; sometimes not.)

Other people feel they have a passion for a career but do not have the skills to convert their passions into earning enough income to support a family with a comfortable middle class lifestyle. People put up roadblocks to their success and are victimized by their own stubbornness of not wanting to "sell out" to a corporate culture. They lose their way to becoming an adult, preferring to think of their image as part of the "rock-and-roll" counterculture. Their sleeve tattoos and body piercings, which looked so cool in their twenties, now brand them in the eyes of perspective employers when they are in their forties. Even if the employers are open to a "rock-and-roll" image, they are concerned their clients might not be.

Whenever you have the opportunity to make a difference, be financially independent, and follow your passion, do so. Your mother has been a good role model for you. She knows she has to live the best life she can, as her mother and I taught her with our actions. She knows she has to be happy for you to be happy.

As you know, your father loves you very much too, and only wants the best for you. Even though your parents chose to divorce each other, they are both forever linked to you. You are part of this family link, and as I see you become an adult, I want you to love your work and develop the necessary skills to parlay your passion into an income which will financially and emotionally support you throughout your life.

# On Effects

———◆———

IN GROWING UP, YOU MAY have the sense that you know yourself, but sometimes, you just don't know what will form you into the person you will become. In assembling the jigsaw puzzle of yourself, you may not quite get how the pieces fit together. The effect of a major event in your life just doesn't have one consequence, but many ricochets, which may determine your future behavior. So it was with the FBI investigations into my parents as suspected security threats to the United States of America.

To reinvent "To His Coy Mistress" by seventeenth-century British poet Andrew Marvel:

> If we had both world and time
> This investigation would be no crime
> But since you drained vital years
> Reducing my innocence to tears—

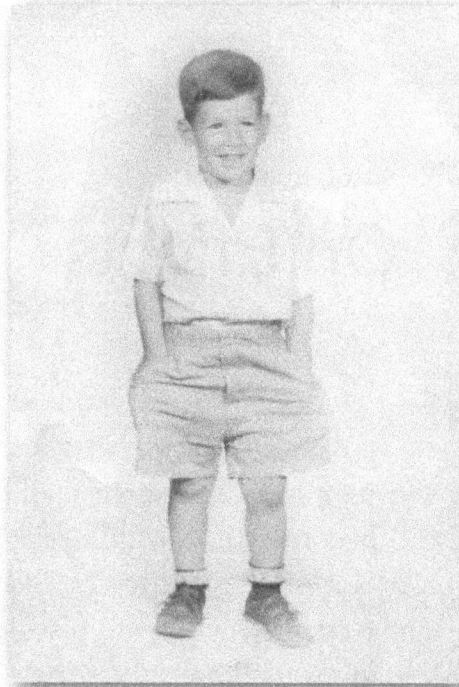

My Boyish Innocence

My mother and my father thought they were shielding me from forces that were trying to destroy our family. It was their protection to build a Chinese wall so that nothing would get through to me. But it did. In many ways, I was that innocent, unnamed child in the FBI reports. Children may not know the specifics of what is wrong, but they can sense the tension all the same, and they know when something is threatening the family that gives them their stability. The incidents in the FBI dossiers were seldom, if ever, talked about in later years.

I have a thousand questions I would like to know the answers to if my parents were alive. I wish I had talked to them more about these investigations when I was in my twenties. I was foolish and in denial, so I didn't.

I was taught to be safe and not become politically active. However, in college and beyond, I attended The March on Washington and believed in Dr. King's vision for racial equality. I protested the Vietnam War, but so did most people who saw that the government was lying to us. My opposition to the war had nothing to do with the brave soldiers who were drafted and served. I admired their service and thought the split between the anti-war and pro-war movement resulted in rhetoric which was polarizing and unnecessary. I was not interested in becoming political.

I did, however, develop a healthy distrust of bureaucracies. It stemmed from the fact that when the FBI New York office told J. Edgar Hoover that my father was not a danger to American security, his response was to disrupt our lives by pressing the Immigration and Naturalization Service to deport my father on "moral" grounds. The bureaucracy just kept churning, without real evidence, to persecute my parents. If you google "Herbert Hoover" and "homosexual," you will find a series of articles alleging Hoover was having an affair with Clyde Tolson, his protege and companion at the FBI. Others alleged that the mob knew this fact and used it to keep Hoover out of their hair. Assuming these allegations are true, how ironic is it that Hoover had my father persecuted for being an "undesirable alien" because he was having relations with my mother out of wedlock, when Hoover was doing the same thing with a man?

According to *The Washington Post*, by the 1960s, the FBI had opened some 432,000 files on "subversive" Americans, with Hoover keeping the most sensitive ones under his personal control. Some of the "subversives" included Supreme Court Justices

Louis Brandeis and Felix Frankfurter, actresses Marilyn Monroe and Mary Pickford, First Lady Eleanor Roosevelt, physicist Albert Einstein, and philanthropist John D. Rockefeller III. My father and mother were in good company.

According to Landon Storrs in *The Oxford Research Encyclopedia*, the government's investigation into a citizen's loyalty resulted in the defendant's inability to earn a living because such economic sanctions were crucial to preserve the status quo and insulate the country from honest dissent. After all, dissent might lead to social and economic reform. For example, in 1947 the FBI hired an additional 7,000 agents to conduct loyalty screenings. In the late 1950s the loyalty program was curbed but the FBI continued to keep files on former loyalty defendants and direct the immigration process to protect American values. People were forced to choose.

Ronald Reagan, our future President, chose to name suspected communists to the House Un-American Activities Committee and continued to earn his livelihood with his successful film career. Dalton Trumbo refused to name names and was blacklisted with a group of screenwriters known as "The Hollywood Ten." The fears which motivated our government bureaucracy to stifle dissent using "guilt by association" are still part of America's underbelly.

The problem is that today we have more sophisticated technology which permeates personal privacy. We have our cellular and data footprints in cyberspace with the National Security Agency (NSA) and other Homeland Security divisions penetrating them in order to keep us safe. It is no longer a guy with a Kodak camera taking pictures of my parents, monitoring our mail, or interviewing our friends, family, and business associates. Edward Snowden in 2013 leaked certain classified information that revealed that the NSA, among various other agencies, had a bulk collection of America's domestic phone records. Though our courts later found this bulk data collection illegal, Snowden was demonized as a traitor under the Espionage Act. His motivation to release the information was that personal privacy was in jeopardy. At 29 years old, he made a decision to spill the beans to the media so people could have a discussion about whether the government should be able to monitor their phones, locations, homes, social media, and personal data.

Powerful players in the Obama administration were both outraged and embarrassed that the government's secret collection of data on U.S. citizens and others had been exposed. It was a simultaneous breach of national security and civil liberties.

As a result of his actions Snowden's life was disrupted; he currently lives in Russia to avoid extradition. If he is a whistleblower who spoke truth to power, what message is the government sending to future whistleblowers? It sort of makes you nostalgic for the good old days when the FBI typed using carbon paper to make copies and the national deportation list was a bunch of index cards. What remains timeless, however, is that the government bureaucracy will promote its own impersonal agenda of secrecy without truly understanding its chilling effects. Demonize first and ask questions later.

My distrust for bureaucracies served me well in my career at the New York City educational system. I did what I had to do so the power structure would leave me alone and let me be creative as a teacher, assistant principal, and principal. Usually this meant making my supervisors look good enough that they would trust my decision-making process and let me do what I needed to do to help my students and staff. In some ways, the New York City educational structure reminds me of the FBI: many people expend a lot of energy without producing much of anything. It is important to be generating papers no matter how repetitive and boring they are. This "paper generation" has an opportunity cost that promotes the status quo while ticking away the time good teachers and supervisors need to create interesting learning environments for their students.

On some level, I was ashamed my parents were investigated. I never knew how to comfortably explain that fact to others. How could I possibly explain the anxiety within me from my parents' histories? If I portrayed the investigations into them as silly, unjust, thoughtless, or a good deal of wasted effort, my protests might fall on deaf ears. My parents were "Pinkos" in a time when it was not easy being pink. I thought it best to avoid the issue. I just wanted to be normal and happy.

I fell in love with my high school sweetheart and married her as soon as I could. I graduated from The State University at Stony Brook in three years to push the marriage process along. I valued my father and mother, who wanted the best for me at every turn. I loved my wife's parents, too, and the idea of a stable nuclear family in spite of the hardships her parents suffered during Hitler's reign in Europe. In a strange way I felt the two families were united by a feeling of persecution, though my wife's family's persecution by Hitler was more severe and life-threatening than the persecution my family faced in the McCarthy era. By comparison, my life was both safe and rich in texture, and in my most difficult moments, I never had to deal with the everyday persecution as my parents and in-laws had thrust upon them. I often reflect on what they experienced and consider that though my daughter or her children will surely face hardships they will have to steel themselves to overcome, they will never have their character tested in the same way as their great-grandparents.

Marriage and family were core to who I was and who I wanted to be. I chose a career in education because I had a passion for teaching and figured it was a safe occupation. I would not be as wealthy as some of my friends and family, but I would have stability, a steady salary, and time to enjoy my life. Those values became ingrained once the FBI knocked on my door. For better or worse, safety was one of the most important things life could offer. I needed something with a sturdy foundation and a roof that would shield me from the harsh elements ever-present in the world and time to which I would be exposed.

In the 1970s, many young families were moving to the "'burbs" for the space and a lifestyle free of the city's grit. Sandy and I tried that move, once looking a "spec" homes near New Marlboro, New Jersey. These were Levittown-like structures with four bedrooms, a sunken living room, modern appliances, and a glorious backyard. They had slab construction with no basement, but they were sleek, beautiful, and a young couple's dream. However, on the reverse commute we got stuck in traffic, and it took us two-and-a-half hours to reach Brooklyn, where we were both employed as teachers. If this time had to be invested in our rush hour commute, we decided to eliminate the suburbs. Finally we bought an old Victorian home built shortly after the turn of the century on Rugby Road. (Coincidentally, two homes down from our house was 1320 Ditmas Avenue, which was the home of film star Mary Pickford, one of the targets of an FBI investigation. She lived there in the 1920s and '30's when she was filming in New York.)

We paid $52,000 and raised Meredith in what the suburbanites referred to as "a neighborhood in transition." Transition was a euphemism for a changing neighborhood which allowed diverse people to own homes previously owned by white people. For us the neighborhood was glorious and seedy all at the same time. Most importantly it had the heterogeneous urban mix in which we wanted to raise our child. It was also a 15-minute commute to work, which gave us the time to be together each day. It was built as a suburb to Manhattan when developers became interested due to the completion of The Brooklyn Bridge in 1882 and The Brighton Subway Line in 1878. By 1908, the Ditmas Park Neighborhood had opened for suburbanites. Today our house would be worth close to $2,000,000. (Ironically, I remember reading that people who had bought the homes in Marlboro were suing the developer because leaks in the roof had allowed the rain water to enter their beautiful sunken living rooms, transforming them into indoor swimming pools. It pays to buy in the suburbs, as long as you pick wisely. Brooklyn was the right "suburban" pick. Even today my daughter wears a gold necklace with "Brooklyn" written across it so that in the upscale, corporate world she manages, she won't forget where she was raised.)

As I put down my homeowner roots, I become the president of the Ditmas Park West neighborhood association to revitalize the neighborhood. We got neighbors taking to each other by closing streets and having concerts and then dealing with substantive neighborhood issues. I was asked to join the Board of Directors of the Flatbush Development Corporation, which improved the housing stock in the area, fought against banks redlining, supported local merchants, and eventually tried to develop the dilapidated Loew's Kings Movie Theater on Flatbush Avenue.

On our block, we made very close friends with three other married couples: Phil and Lani Tama, Ofra and Jeff Werden, and Cheryl Parker and Dave Ford. We shared our time together using our porches, backyard, and large homes as gathering places to enjoy our friendship. Then time came and first took Ofra with cancer and then Lani. Cheryl had a bout with breast cancer, too, but survived. Eventually she and David divorced. Time had interceded and we had no choice but to deal with the losses.

By 1989, we decided to build a vacation home in the Berkshires. We needed a place where we could go to escape the pressures of work and be open to different vistas. The home was in a community called Indian Lake because the bank that had developed the property thought it would be a bright idea to name each dirt road after a different Native American tribe. Down the road, there was another community named Sherwood Forest, which had had the bright idea of naming streets after Robin Hood and his merry men. Indian Lake, which is man-made, has three beaches, a pond, two tennis courts, and miles of dirt roads lined with trees you could walk like Henry David Thoreau, another Berkshire resident.

We hired one of the best builder/craftsman to construct our passive solar house with a study basement and protective roof with a view where all you could see were trees. The lot had old stone walls that had been used as corrals when the property was part of a sheep farm. At the bottom of the lot was a babbling brook and as a result we had deer, bears, raccoons, porcupines, wild turkeys, and foxes all visible from our living room windows. Our grandchildren named our home "The Tree House" because with the walkout basement was underneath the living room and main deck, which in turn elevated them to be in the trees.

Indian Lake was rural and at least 20 minutes to anywhere, which for me gave it an appeal. Some people in the community vehemently objected to putting up a "STOP" sign on Moberg Road, where it intersected with the paved town road of Bonny Rigg Hill, because it was too urban for them. I should mention that Moberg is the one street in the community not named after a Native American tribe but rather for the family who had the sheep farm. I can say this fact with some certainty because I googled Moberg Indians, and there were no hits on any such Jewish tribe.

When at Indian Lake, I learned to love the activities. I would swim across the lake, counting each stroke until I reached the safety of the beach. I bought a canoe and fished a catch and release protocol to my heart's content, landing pickerel, bass, pike, perch, and sunnies. My tennis improved; I still enjoy singles. I learned late in life to ski and can do black diamond trails. I am now learning golf after years of resisting because I wasn't old or boring enough to play. I learned more about classical music at Tanglewood than I ever thought I would. The theaters, while not Broadway, have interesting moments, and the dance at Jacob's Pillow can challenge my thought processes, as can the MASS MoCa or The Clark museum.

However, it is not the activities that give this place its value. It is the friends I have acquired, many of them from the Indian Lake community. After my wife's death, there was a group of friends who gave me their time and caring to help me through the grieving process. These friendships are what make time valuable.

Now that I am in a relationship with Joan, it is interesting to me how much she sees the Berkshires as part of my personality. Her friends, concerned with her welfare, were of the opinion if you live with a man it should be on neutral grounds and not in the house of his departed wife. I don't see my house in that way. It is a place I can easily share with Joan because I love her. My late wife and her late husband will always be part of our lives, but they are separate entities from our connection together. She was strong enough to be with me in the Berkshires against her friend's advice. She bonds with my friends, and they enjoy her. I tease her that they enjoy her more than they do me. The street is not one-way, and I certainly do socialize with her friends, which are twice as numerous as mine. Maybe at some point I will sell the house and move on, but for now, the foundation is sturdy and the roof is solid.

# On Love

---

NOT TO LOVE IS ONE of life's greatest tragedies. The isolation devastates the human spirit. Yet so many people are afraid to love or simply do not know how. Audrey Hepburn, one of my favorite actors, defined love as "holding onto each other."

Sandy as a Columbia
University Ph.D. Grad

I held onto my first wife Sandy, and she to me, for as long as we could. After meeting in high school and knowing each other for over 50 years, she told me on her deathbed that "she could have not done better." She hugged me and held me close in that lucid moment. I knew she was right because I could not have done any better, either. It was a complete marriage and love affair all in one neat package. It was the type of marriage in which we could complete each other's sentences, share a career as teachers, assistant principals, and principals together, and produce a daughter, Meredith, who has evolved into one of the best people parents' could ever hope to have.

After Sandy passed on—having gone from a bright, alert, physically active person to an invalid in just 40 days—I felt betrayed by an end-of-life hospital system in America which preys off the next procedure to prolong life instead of understanding the patient's explicit wishes for a "good death." In the most difficult decision of our lives, Meredith and I had to intervene and advocate for Sandy's death, as stated in her living will, to doctors who wanted to prolong her life with unproven experimental treatments. These treatments piqued their medical curiosity but in effect would have diminished Sandy's capacity to live a life she would have wanted to live.

Alone and devastated by the loss, I spent the next six months of my life in grief therapy trying to figure out if it was possible to move on. During that time I wrote my first book, *The Grievance: A Real Life-and-Death Story*, which described Sandy's legacy to my grandchildren. They would read this book when they were old enough to learn her life's lessons. The writing helped immensely and gave me a purpose to move forward. It also helped readers understand that the end-of-life system practiced in America's hospitals must be reformed to value a patient's quality of life above all else. My daughter, family, and friends built a small, intricate cocoon around me, woven with threads of kindness.

I had many talks with my daughter, who at this pivotal time came to the realization that her marriage was not making her happy and that even with two children she loved dearly, there were not enough solid building blocks to right the structure. She went to marriage counseling and then mediation with her husband, and fortunately they both decided to end the marriage and do what was necessary to stabilize their two wonderful children.

She and I simultaneously entered new phases of our lives. I had told her that I thought I needed a relationship to be happy but had no idea how find love again. I didn't even think it was possible to do so. After all, the last time I had dated was in high school, and I didn't think my knowledge of *Sgt. Pepper's Lonely Hearts Club Band* would sustain me through a first date.

Then fate struck me. Without the assistance of JDate, eHarmony, or any other electronic matchmakers, I met someone in my bereavement at the 92nd Street Y. Joan was a year younger than me and had lost the love of her life, Alan, to a 15-year struggle with leukemia. Alan had managed commercial and industrial real estate on Long Island.

Like Sandy and I, Joan and Alan had met in high school and were grounded by their family and friends. In the last year of his illness, Alan underwent an intense struggle to survive during his second stem cell procedure until the disease overpowered him. Joan, out of love, compassion, and necessity, became the anchor to help her family to persevere. As she spoke to the group, I saw the sadness in her grief but that she had a warm and welcoming spirit. She had humor in describing her family and seven grandchildren, three by her daughter Lizzie and four by her son David. I could tell by her descriptions that their spouses, Adam and Dara, also meant the world to her, as did each of her grandchildren.

Joan was an elementary school teacher in Brentwood who loved her job and felt that the largely disadvantaged children in her class deserved the best education she could give them. She grew up in Rockville Center, Long Island where her father was a car dealer and her mother was a housewife. She was the oldest child with one sister and brother. Once married, she moved to Roslyn where she raised her children and formed a wide circle of very loyal friends. In short, she knew how to nurture people, and I was attracted to her grace and style.

At first Joan and I were only entertaining the idea of companionship, where we might date occasionally and enjoy New York City together. I really don't know how I fell in love with her, but I did, as she did with me. I think, in part, it was that we both had histories of knowing how to develop and sustain relationships. We went from dating each other to spending weeks together on her turf in Boca Raton, Florida or my turf in San Miguel de Allende, Mexico. It just seemed natural that we live together, and we decided to do so.

In our love, there is the kind of physical attraction where your heart beats quicker when the other person is near. More importantly, there is an emotional bond where you can feel safe with your lover because you share similar values. Money, greed, mistrust, and power are what destroys many relationships. Joan and I are in the same economic bracket; we do not need to be financially dependent on each other. We can trust each other. If there is anything we do not understand, we can talk freely about it.

At the start of our relationship, good friends on each side worried that we were simply "on the rebound." However, to find true love, you need to use your head as well as your heart. Neither Joan nor I felt we were replacing the other's spouse. We talk about our first spouses freely. We were lucky that we were able to love deeply again even after we thought those chapters of our lives were finished. We want to hold onto each other, and for us, that gives our life a new meaning.

# On Loss

———◆———

LOSS IS A FEELING OF grief that you have when deprived of someone or something you value. Everyone experiences it at one time
or another.

You valued your grandmother because she loved you so purely, as
only a grandmother can. Yet she died unexpectedly, only to leave
you with your memories in her absence.

You have experienced your parents go through a process of separation and divorce, leaving you at times sad, confused, angry, and
stressed. "Why can't things be like the way they were before?" you
have asked with tears in your eyes.

On August 7, 2005, on your parents' wedding day, I made the following toast: "What greater thing is there for two human souls
than to feel they are joined for life—to strengthen each other
as they proceed on life's voyage, to laugh with each other, to
strengthen each other in times of sorrow, to be one with each
other in memories of a rich, full life."

Little did I know, ten years later, they would be filing for a divorce. It seems that for whatever reasons, they eventually did not strengthen each other or make each other laugh. In the end, it was probably better that they decided to separate in such a way that they could love you the way children deserve to be loved. One fact is undeniable: Things can no longer be the way they were.

Sometimes I wish I could make time stand still where happiness and tranquility radiate in everything we see and do. Even though I am your Poppy, I do not have these powers, and even if I did, using them would stop you from growing up to be strong, capable, and ready to take on life. To understand how to cope with loss will give you resilience. In a divorce, there are a few simple things for you to understand.

There is nothing you could have done to prevent your parents from separating. Their separation is not your fault. They both continue to love you very much and want you to be confident and strong. They both will give you routines and structures so that you have a sense of stability whether you are at Mommy's house or Daddy's house. You must express your feelings to them and give Mommy and Daddy a chance to acknowledge them. How well you understand and express your hopes, fears, needs, and wants will help them see you through your eyes, not theirs. Hug them whenever you can and stay physically close. I know it is not easy for you to deal with loss.

To help you, I am going to tell you a story. It is not my story, but one by Sandra Cisneros, a favorite author of mine who wrote

*The House on Mango Street.* It is an allegory called *Have You Seen Marie?*

The story features two girls, Sandra and Roz, and Roz's black-and-white cat, Marie. When Sandra's mother dies, Marie—who is a symbol of loss—disappears. Sandra and Roz set out to find her in their San Antonio neighborhood in an attempt to stabilize themselves in the face of enormous grief over the death of Sandra's mother. In their search, they meet all kinds of interesting people who are open to helping them find Marie but who suffer from various afflictions, quirks, and losses of their own. It is only when Sandra openly expresses her pain at the loss of her mother, connects with the natural world around her, and finds a way to carry her mother's essence with her in life that Marie reappears.

In Mexico some people believe that what was lost will gradually come back within you if you are open enough to let it happen. It is a rebirth, but it will not be in the same form as it was before. It will have to be nurtured and handled with care. The question for you is: Are they right, and if they are, how will you fill the void of your losses to give you strength?

One in two marriages in America end in divorce. As reported in the British newspaper *The Guardian* on November 22, 2015, out of 514 young people interviewed, ages 14-22 with long-term cohabiting relationships, 82% of children of divorced couples think their living situation improved once their parents were divorced. Feelings of guilt and confusion are natural part of the process.

The article goes on to state that children want to see their parents acting responsibly—for example, not arguing in front of them.

If you first acknowledge and accept the loss, positive things may happen. You may discover coping strategies to make you more resilient. You may develop increased empathy for others since you will understand there are different points of view. You may become more self-sufficient and understand how intricate a marriage can be. Finally, if your parents co-parent well, as I am sure they will, you may have more quality time with each parent.

Given time, sometimes the emptiness of a loss can be filled with the stuff that makes your life richer. You may not accept this premise now, but it is my hope that someday you will.

# On Escape

———◆———

Escapism is defined by *The Psychology Dictionary* as "the tendency a person has to escape from the real world to one of delight or security." I have found that in order to maintain your balance, sometimes it is necessary to leave the routines of everyday life when they become boring or arduous. Disassociations for limited periods of time can revitalize the soul.

People usually think escape means running away from something; if it does, it is a feeble escape, because that something will always have faster gait than you. For me, escape is running to some place where I can release my mind from everyday pressures and let my creative thoughts soar. It is finding the right entertainment or activities to complement your life. Everyone needs to escape. Choose your venues wisely. Invariably your escapes will weave themselves back into your life in ways you won't be able to predict.

Movies are what provide me a safe haven. I can go into a dark theater and watch miracles projected on a large screen. I can see vast vistas contrasted by a quick wince of an eye entrapping me in the character's story. I remember marveling at Orson Welles

1941 masterpiece *Citizen Kane* when the last word out of Charles Foster Kane's mouth at the beginning of the movie was "rosebud." Kane was modeled on the life of William Randolph Hearst, the famous newspaper publisher who practiced "yellow journalism" to manipulate his readers to support the Spanish-American War. It is a cautionary tale of what money, power, and prestige can do to people in America.

In 1942, Michael Curtiz directed *Casablanca* with Humphrey Bogart and Ingrid Bergman in a grade-B thriller that resonated because of the universals of love and morality as you rooted for Rick, the anti-hero, to make things right in a world where Nazis were pulling the strings. In 1993, Steven Spielberg directed *Schindler's List* starring Liam Neeson as Oskar Schindler, a German businessman in Poland who employed Jews in his plant. It is one of the best American-made Holocaust films in which righteous action triumphs of the evils of Nazism. When you watch it, your great-grandparents may be watching it with you. Finally, in 1939, Victor Fleming directed *The Wizard of Oz* starring Judy Garland, Ray Bolger, and Bert Lahr. I saw it as a seven-year-old child at the Linden Theater on Rodgers Avenue in Brooklyn—and cried hysterically because those flying monkeys were the scariest creatures I had ever seen. It was a child's fantasy, rich with color, song, characters, imagination, and heart.

In the 1990s, when I became a founding assistant principal at The High School for Telecommunications (which replaced the failing Bay Ridge High School), I had the freedom to create more meaningful academic courses. As an elective, I developed the interdisciplinary course titled "Social Cinema" in which great films were analyzed for their social significance. It became one of the most popular electives in the school. It opened up the world and its issues for my students in a way the regurgitating textbooks could not.

Theater also provided an escape for me. In 1958, when I was twelve years old, my mother took me to see *West Side Story* on Broadway. I was hooked on the theatrical magic I witnessed that day. The Sharks and Jets on the streets of Manhattan were embroiled in the same Romeo-and-Juliet story of Shakespeare's, but with Leonard Bernstein's music, Stephen Sondheim's lyrics, Jerome Robbins's direction. I was mesmerized for the three hours and never wanted its beauty to end. In 1962, I went to see Edward Albee's *Who's Afraid of Virginia Woolf* directed by Mike Nichols. The brutal absurdity of George and Martha's marriage as played out in mind games with a second couple, Nick and Honey, showed frail relationships which float between reality and illusion.

In 1984, I saw the revival of Arthur Miller's *Death of A Salesman*, starring Dustin Hoffman, a play that originally premiered on Broadway in 1949. The play questions the American Dream and whether it is attainable as Willie Loman, the main character lives somewhere between reality and his memories. Does capitalism work in providing opportunity or is it flawed, selling dreams that are hollow?

In 2012, I saw the musical *The Book of Mormon* by Trey Parker, Robert Lopez, and Matt Stone. It is a satire of religion where two

Mormon missionaries are selected to go to a remote Ugandan village to convert the "natives" who have more pressing problems like AIDS, famine, and violence. When it works, live performance just sucks you onto the stage, captures your thoughts and won't release them until you see the world differently.

There was one point in my life when I was at New York University's Graduate School. After receiving a Master of Arts degree in history, I wasn't sure what to do so I decided to go for a Doctorate in history. It bored me. I decided instead to switch to the Theater program at The Tisch School for The Preforming Arts. I earned a Master of Arts Degree in theater, and it was one of the best decisions I ever made. It opened up worlds. What I learned about becoming a good teacher did not come from any of my education courses. It came from the knowledge of how to put a story across with words and movement designed to engage audiences.

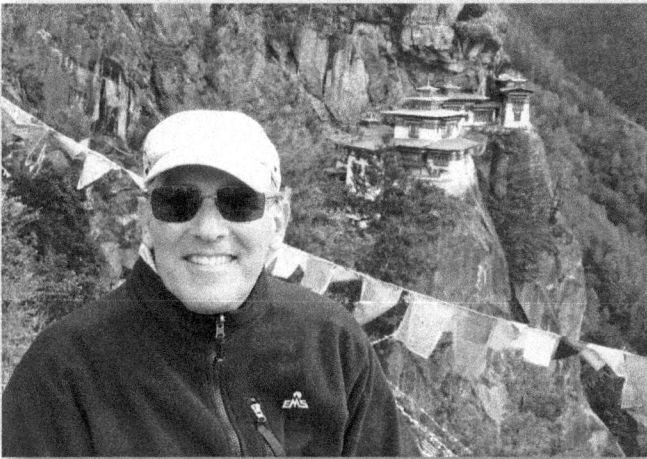

Larry in Bhutan

Even beyond offering escape, travel teaches you who you are. The more travel you do, the more you will have to grapple with who you are and why the world is the way it is. It teaches you independence because you are removed from your support systems and have to make decisions about how to get from place to place safely. It shows you a world which is quite different from the one into which you were born. You question what your life might be like were it not for the fortunate accident of birth where you emerged a middle-class environment in New York City.

Some of the stupidest advice I ever received was by the assistant principal of social studies at my first teaching job at Sheepshead Bay High School. Looking at my program for the year, I had been given non-western civilization classes to teach to the ninth graders. I had next to no academic training in non-western courses and had no idea how to proceed. The supervisor told me, "A good teacher can teach anything. Just follow the textbooks." I later found out he said that because the senior teachers in his department hated teaching non-western civilization and he had to convince newbies like me it was teachable. I did follow the textbooks, and what I didn't know and couldn't explain after reading them would fill the ancient libraries in both Sankore Madrasah, Timbuktu and Ephesus, Turkey.

In my journey to try to comprehend the intricacies of foreign cultures, I decided to travel. I just had a curiosity to know what I didn't know. Once I achieved a more sophisticated level of understanding the world, I would know better how to teach it in a classroom. I have visited over 100 countries, some just on vacation and some as a Freeman Foundation Scholar, doing in-depth research and then traveling with colleagues to places like China, Japan, Tibet, Mongolia, and Korea. I learned that life on our planet is far more intricate than what is portrayed in textbooks.

Lisa See, author of *Sunflower and the Secret Fan*, also had a passion for travel. At a writer's conference in San Miguel de Allende, she spoke of her desire to visit a place in remote China where women had developed their own secret language called "nu shu" as a way to maintain their traditions in a society which forbids them to obtain an education and binds their feet as objects of beauty. Her curiosity compelled her to undertake this extensive journey to a remote village accompanied by her guide. There was a welcoming dinner where it would have been considered bad manners not to partake in the carefully prepared local delicacies. She did and at one point asked her guide what see was eating. "Pig penis," he responded. You may be wondering, what does pig penis taste like? According the Lisa See, it tastes just like chicken.

In my travels, I have not eaten pig penis, but I have had rooster testicles, rattlesnake, fried grasshoppers, roasted guinea pig, kudu, yak milk, and bat. Except for the grasshoppers and yak milk, the rest do taste like chicken. I did not set out to eat them, but somehow it seemed like the thing to do at the time. If you push your boundaries, you will expand and do things you never thought it would be possible to do. I have slid down a mountain of snow and ice in Antarctica; snorkeled in the South Pacific; watched geysers erupt in Chile's Atacama Dessert; had tea with the near-extinct Reindeer people in Mongolia; participated in the Toraja people's burial ceremony in Sulewasi, Indonesia as they slit their cattles' throats to send the departed souls to the after-life; sat with Buddhist monks seeking freedom from oppression in Myanmar; walked through Masai villages in Kenya; and toured Dharavi, the slums of Mumbai, India and its Brazilian equivalent, the Favelas. It all wasn't rugged, third-world travel. I have been to some of the best restaurants and vineyards in Australia, New Zealand, South Africa, Chile, Argentina, Spain, Italy, and France.

You need to find your personal balance as to what is comfortable and uncomfortable. Too many people experience "culture shock" and suddenly become confused and anxious when exposed to different cultures. As a result, they decide to hide within themselves and in doing so ignore what is real. Your passport is now unstamped. My wish is you fill it up with wonder and travel wherever and whenever you can.

Life becomes a balancing act between freedom and discipline. Most people think they are two different concepts but, in reality, they are complementary. Freedom and discipline need each other's parameters in order to exist. The lessons in this book have these forces in their subtext. To achieve your potential you must be free to attain a good life and have the structure to maintain it for you and your children. Once you do, it will be your turn to pass your life's lessons—your legacy of how best to live—to your children, knowing full well that they will change based on circumstances and translation.

My wish is that like your great-grandparents, grandmother, and mother before you, you will live free and live with purpose to achieve a good life. Have the discipline and courage to make right what goes wrong. The preceding pages bear tales of the courage to discover happiness and find it where it is already present within you. As your grandfather, there is no greater gift I can bestow.

# Epilogue

—

As our life lessons come to a close, I would like to leave you with a quote from "Jabberwocky" by Lewis Carroll, a poet who could make sense out of nonsense.

"The time has come," the Walrus said,
"To talk of many things:
Of shoes—and ships—and sealing-wax—
Of cabbages—and kings—
And why the sea is boiling hot—
And whether pigs have wings."

"But wait a bit," the Oysters cried,
"Before we have our chat;
For some of us are out of breath,
And all of us are fat!"
"No hurry!" said the Carpenter.
They thanked him much for that.

So, if by reading this book you find yourself out of breath or fat, remember there is no hurry to become who you are.

At the *bris* of a newborn Jewish son, the *mohel*, who performed the circumcision on the baby boy, held up a beautiful, richly knotted, and browned loaf of challah. Ordinarily I have a natural fear of *mohels* and have always kept a safe distance except once when I was too young to know any better; however, this *mohel* drew me in with the following story. The raw materials compose the bread, but they are not the bread. They are unformed like a baby with endless potential. To create challah, you must take time with the ingredients, mixing warm water with yeast, and adding flour, honey, vegetable oil, eggs, salt, and poppy seeds. You must knead the dough carefully into braided knots, brush it with an egg wash, and bake it at 375 degrees. Only with love and care will the challah form into a thing of beauty.

So it is with a child. Take the time to get your recipe just right so you can savor each taste that life offers.

# A Challenge to Readers

———

THE COVER OF *TWENTY LIFE Lessons* is clouds at sunset. I have always been mesmerized by sunsets. I have experienced them throughout the world—how the clouds in the sky reflect the sun's aura. Across the globe, people have a common reaction. They are stunned and inspired by the beauty the light casts onto our world. For that reason, sunsets are the most commonly photographed event in nature.

At sunset you can relax and behold the overwhelming spectacle that surrounds you. You think, reflect and reach a state of calm. In twilight, there is clarity. A young Joni Mitchell, in her iconic song "Both Sides Now," sings:

> I've looked at clouds from both sides now,
> from up and down, and still somehow
> it's cloud illusions I recall.
> I really don't know clouds at all.

Aging, if done well, allows you to separate illusions from reality. The wisdom to envision truths and share your life lessons with the ones you love frees you. It is a time of life when you understand clouds, their mysteries and predicaments.

In combining memories with teachable moments, *Twenty Life Lessons* in a non-sequential memoir. It is a translatable format designed for people who wish to tell their stories to their children and grandchildren. Each reader will undoubtedly have his or her own life lessons. My hope is that after reading this book, readers will be inspired to tell their stories in the form of life lessons. Such is the stuff that sunsets are made of.

www.ingramcontent.com/pod-product-compliance
Lightning Source LLC
LaVergne TN
LVHW011242080426
835509LV00005B/599